How to Write Excellent Law Essays

An Unorthodox Guide

Dr. Dimitrios Kyriazis

Copyright © 2024 by Dr. Dimitrios Kyriazis

All rights reserved. This book or any portion thereof may not be reproduced or used in any manner whatsoever without the express written permission of the publisher except for the use of brief quotations in a book review.

Contents

Introduction — v

Chapter 1:
Who gets the best marks? — 1

Chapter 2:
The purpose of an essay — 4

Chapter 3:
Alexander the Great, Sherlock Homes and
Law Essay Writing — 6

Chapter 4:
Essay Introduction (and opening lines...) — 10

Chapter 5:
How to Argue — 16

Chapter 6:
The Main Body of the Essay — 24

Chapter 7:
Essay Conclusions — 33

Chapter 8:
(Re)writing like Hemingway — 36

Chapter 9:
Revision Strategy — 38

Chapter 10:
Comparison is the thief of joy								40

Chapter 11:
Academic feedback and how to receive it						41

Chapter 12:
Managing Expectations								44

Chapter 13:
General Essay Writing Advice							46

Chapter 14:
Guest contribution by Lord Neuberger						54

Chapter 15:
Guest contribution by Professor Nick Barber					56

Chapter 16:
Guest contribution by Professor Mark Elliott					61

Chapter 17:
Guest contribution by Professor Alison Young					67

Chapter 18:
Guest contribution by Professor David Kershaw					73

Chapter 19:
Guest contribution by Professor Joanne van der Leun				75

Chapter 20:
Guest contribution by Professor Catherine Barnard				78

Chapter 21:
Guest contribution by Professor Stephen Weatherill				82

Chapter 22:
Conclusion: It's not all about the marks						85

Chapter 23:
About the Author									87

Introduction

This book is for eveyrone interested in improving their essay writing skills. It is focused on law essays, but the principles discussed here apply to essay writing in general. It is written with the purpose of assisting law students in navigating the very stressful periods of exams and other summative or formative assessments. Treat it like a guide, but feel free to diverge at times, when you feel that a certain piece of advice does not suit your needs.

I would like to thank all contributors for the excellent advice they have shared with us. It is a great privilege for law students to be able to receive advice from luminaries such as Baron Neuberger, former President of the UK Supreme Court, Professor Mark Elliott (Chair of the Faculty of Law at the University of Cambridge), Oxford Law Professor Nick Barber, Oxford Law Professor (Emeritus) Stephen Weatherill, Cambridge Law Professor Alison Young, Cambridge Law Professor Catherine Barnard, Professor David Kershaw (Dean of the LSE Law School) and Professor van der Leun (former Dean of Leiden Law School). I am deeply indebted to them.

It is common for a law student to feel lost when first asked to produce a law essay, especially within a tight timeframe. They do not know how to start, what to read, how to write... Sometimes they do not even really know what is actually expected of them! With marking criteria being rather vague (and rarely being oserved), and with marking itself being more of an art than a science, unpredictability reins supreme. This should not be the norm. This book aims to change this and equip law student with an autopilot of sorts that allows them to navigate tricky legal terrain.

The topics covered by this book are, inter alia, the following. First, how to dissect essay questions and essay promopts. Second, how to identify the keywords in the prompt and question. Third, how to unpack a question's underlying assumption(s). Fourth, how to create a succinct introduction, built around paraphrasing adn arguing. Fifth, how to create a compelling argument. Sixth, how to try and balance primary and secondary sources properly. Seventh, how to conclude.

If you wish to stay up-to-date with new content on legal essay writing, kindly subscribe to my blog at https://www.thelawprof.com/. I hope you will enjoy reading this book as much as I enjoyed writing it.

This book is dedicated to all law students, but especially the stressed-out ones; this one is for you!

Best of luck with your writing,
Dimitrios Kyriazis,
DPhil (Oxford University)

CHAPTER 1

Who gets the best marks?

It used to be an enigma for me. Why did Eric or Jessica get a distinction in the mock exam, while my performance was rather mediocre? They must have studied a lot more! Worse still, they must be super clever, something I can do nothing about... Or, they just practised exam writing for tens of hours. They did something right and I did something wrong.

You will have heard the following complaint from fellow students, your tutees or even from your past self: "I studied so hard, why didn't I do well in the exam?".

Another iteration of this would be "I always read everything on the reading list, why are my essay marks not improving?".

The assumption underlying such questions is simple: knowledge of the law, whether that be case law or statutes or academic textbooks, is enough in order to grant a student access to excellent marks.

This assumption is, simply put, false.

Knowledge of the law is surely the most self-evident ingredient to success. If you have not studied, if you do not have a solid grasp of the key primary and secondary sources, you will not excel.

However, the key thing to remember here is that it is only ONE of the ingredients to success.

On its own, knowledge of the law is necessary in order to succeed, but not sufficient.

In summative assessments, the student that does well is not the student who studied the most, but the student who managed to correctly apply her legal knowledge to the exam question, while properly managing time and stress.

In other words: please do study, but do not rely on your knowledge of the law alone to carry you though. This makes no more sense than relying on your endurance and strength to carry you through a boxing match. You must actually master the art of boxing, and similarly you must master the art of essay writing and the art of answering exam questions. This book is one of the many resources available to help you.

Knowing how to draft good legal essays is a complex skill that few students master. Let's see why, and how you can be one of the select few. But first…a few words about tennis!

The Inner Game of Exams

In 1972, Timothy Gallwey published a book entitled "The Inner Game of Tennis".

The book was a runaway success, receiving dithyrambic reviews. I highly recommend you read it.

It is hardly about tennis; its main thesis is of more general application and is quite interesting indeed. If it sounds self-evident today, it is partly due to Gallwey's contribution. Here it is:

"It is the thesis of this book that neither mastery nor satisfaction can be found in the playing of any game without giving some attention to the relatively neglected skills of the inner game. This is the game that takes place in the mind of the player, and it is played against such obstacles as lapses in concentration, nervousness, self-doubt, and self-condemnation. In short, it is played to overcome all habits of mind which inhibit excellence in performance."

These dicta, in my view, apply to exams as well, which is why I gave this section the title "The Inner Game of Exams".

When it comes to sitting an exam, you can be your own worst enemy, even if you are very well prepared. Sometimes, especially when you are very well prepared.

You start doubting yourself. You think that the question cannot possibly ask what you think it asks, since you understood it relatively easily. Surely, it shouldn't have been that easy for you to understand?

Your heart starts racing. The examinees around you are writing like maniacs. You are off to a slow start. Surely, they must know more than you since they started answering straight away? Surely, the student that starts answering first must possess an advantage?

Everything is suddenly magnified. "I will not do well in this exam. I will fail all my exams! I should have never entered law school. I will never become a lawyer anyway. What was I thinking?"

An avalanche of self-doubt creeps in just because you succumbed to a nanosecond of doubt.

It does not have to be this way.

Before each and every exam, try to put things in perspective. What's the worst case scenario, really? Not in theory, e.g. Armageddon, but in reality, personally for you? You will soon realise, it's not that bad after all.

As I write in my free PDF guide, which you can get by inserting your email address at the bottom of the homepage or on the landing page:

"In summative assessments the student that does well is not necessarily the student who studied the most, but the student who managed to correctly apply her legal knowledge to the exam question, while properly managing time and stress."

Slowly and steadily, try to become that person. Your course leaders are there to help you. Time is your ally. Keep calm and practice!

CHAPTER 2

The purpose of an essay

The word essay comes to us from French, and the root verb means "to try". That's all that is asked of you: to try! To give it your best shot, to try to answer the exam question to the best of your abilities.

What is the purpose of an essay? Persuasion. You need to convince the essay reader, in your case the marker and/or course leader for your course, that you have actually mastered the material they taught you. Achieve this, and an excellent mark is yours. If you can persuade them that their teaching, their seminars, their slides, their carefully drafted exam questions were not in vain, then your essay (your try, your effort) will not be in vain either.

So, keep this in mind. The goal is not a Distinction. The goal is persuasion; the Distinction will necessarily follow.

Since your essay is most probably going to be marked by your course leader, or at least by someone else in accordance with the course leader's instructions, you need to speak to them through your essay.

I know that what I am about to say will sound harsh but it is the truth, unless you are studying at a university where a big chunk of your final mark is dependent on class participation or other extra-exam activities. No one cares about what you know. No one cares about whether you remembered all the case law a day before the exam. No one cares about what you meant to say! No one cares about the fact that all your fellow students came to you for advice the week leading up to the exam. No one cares about you always participating in class and asking intelligent questions.

All that matters is: on the day of the exam, did you perform? What did you actually write? What made it to your exam script and in what form? What did you ACTUALLY write, not what did you MEAN to write. Only results matter.

Please keep in mind something else, too. This is crucial. Sounds a bit unfair, but it is true and should be used to your advantage. Marking is an art, not a science. Despite all the detailed grading schemes and the elaborate assessment criteria, two excellent markers can disagree on the appropriate mark for an exam script. And they can both somehow be right! Marking is an art. It is not an exact science.

This brings me to another point. I always tell my students: excellent marks are stolen, not given. This usually baffles them. What I mean is less mysterious than it might seem, i.e. all I mean is that a marker does not so much consciously decide to hand a student an excellent mark, but feels like their exam script deserves nothing but an excellent mark. It is like a feeling, not a conscious decision (usually, at least). You feel that this student deserves an excellent mark based on the quality of their submitted work, and that's it. All you know need to decide is how excellent the mark is going to be, if they will be recommended for a prize etc etc. But the distinction question is settled: this script has to get a distinction.

So, my advice to you, quoting Steve Martin: be so good theuy can't ignore you. Perform so well that the marker will have no option but to give you a distinction. In fighting terms, don't let the fight go to the judges' scorecards: secure the knockout and settle this fight yourself.

CHAPTER 3

Alexander the Great, Sherlock Homes and Law Essay Writing

Alexander the Great

"The principles of Caesar were those of Hannibal, and those of Hannibal were those of Alexander: keeping your forces together, not being vulnerable at any point, rapidly bringing all your forces to bear on a given point."

This is a quote by Napoleon Bonaparte, as published in an excellent compilation of his aphorisms and thoughts by French novelist Honoré de Balzac.

Although it concerns war, this quote can be used in an academic context as well (aka the war-place of ideas). Let us attempt to dissect it and apply its teachings in the context of drafting an argumentative legal essay.

Keeping your forces together

Every law essay, every piece of legal writing in general, ought (in principle) to be argumentative. The essay, moreover, needs to be bound by a single argumentative thread. Even you veer from the topic to make a point or cite some relevant research, it all need to come back to what you are trying to "prove", i.e. to your central thesis. Your "forces", therefore, i.e. your paragraphs and your various sub-arguments, need to stay close together. Too many sprinkles of irrelevant ideas, too many parantheses, too many historical facts, and the thread is cut; the essay is no longer forceful enough, no longer convincing. Focus, focus, focus and stick to the script.

Not being vulnerable at any point

This is the other side of the coin. Sure, you need to be very solid at one point (your central thesis). Still, the even harder part is that you are not allowed to have any real weaknesses anywhere else, i.e. any real argumentative vulnerabilities. As the saying goes: "Offence wins games but defence wins championships". This is true for both basketball games and law essays. An essay with a brilliant point and a compelling argument will rapidly unravel if some paragraphs are so weak they seem to have been written by a different author. In other words: try to write in a way that is intelligent, in part by avoiding writing in a way that is simplistic.

Swift and concentrated action at the critical point

This is, perhaps, the hardest part. You have helped your reader navigate all sides of the argument, while politely but assertively steering them your way. You have escaped major pitfalls and minimised your vulnerabilities. Now what?

Now is the time for you to bring your point home. Towards the end of your essay (or the end of your piece of writing in general) you need all your previously developed arguments to crescendo together, demonstrating why your position is clearly the most compelling of all the alternatives. The way the essay reaches this critical point will determine whether you "win" or "lose", whether the reader is sold or not. Granted, the stakes cannot be compared with Alexander's cavalry charge against Darius in Gaugamela, but bringing your forces to bear on your key point will be equally decisive in the context of your writing.

To sum up, three takeaways emerge from the stratagems of the great Greek commander, as synopsised by Napoleon: focus on your strengths, avoid major vulnerabilities and strike forcefully when the time is right. Fortune favours the bold, the decisive, the argumentative.

Sherlock Holmes

[Scotland Yard detective]: Is there any other point to which you would wish to draw my attention?

Holmes: To the curious incident of the dog in the night-time.

[Scotland Yard detective]: The dog did nothing in the night-time.

Holmes: That was the curious incident.

In his short story "The Adventure of Silver Blaze", Sir Arthur Conan Doyle presents his protagonist, Sherlock Holmes, with a seemingly impenetrable mystery. Silver Blaze, a famous race horse, disappears on the eve of an important race, and its trainer is found murdered. Scotland Yard arrests a bookmaker as the primary suspect, but Holmes is not convinced.

After a meandering and captivating narration, a key element that helps Holmes reach a solution is the "curious incident of the dog in the night-time". The dog that was present in the scene at the time of the murder did not bark. As Holmes explained, he immediately grasped the significance of its silence. The only possible inference was that the murderer was someone the dog knew well. The mystery was soon solved and the horse safely returned to its owner.

What inference can we, now, draw from this story in relation to legal essay writing?

In my view, the key takeaway here is the need to pay attention to negative cues. The average student, and person for that matter, does not generally heed negative cues. Instead of focusing on the things that should have happened, but did not happen, we tend to focus on "positive" information, namely on what actually happened.

This perfectly natural tendency might be limiting our essay writing progress. Using the modus cogitandi of Sherlock Holmes, we could mobilise our imagination in order to pay attention to what is missing.

For instance: what is the essay question not asking? What information is missing from the essay prompt? Was this omitted on purpose? Is it, or could it be argued to be, significant? Furthermore, what is this secondary source (e.g. a monograph) not mentioning? What did the Supreme Court judges not comment on? What negative cues can we use in order to construct a more compelling argument?

Sometimes, absence can be as significant as presence. Dr Watson had complimented Holmes on his masterful deductions by saying that he had rendered detection as near an exact science as it ever would be rendered in this world. It is worth examining what we stand to gain by applying a similar line of reasoning to legal essay writing.

CHAPTER **4**

Essay Introduction (and opening lines...)

The beginning is half of everything, as the great Greek Plato used to say. How you start your essays is the single most important determinant of your marks. First impressions do matter! So, my goal in this chapter is twofold.

One, I want to teach you the way I found most effective in getting excellent marks. As a law student in Oxford who gratuated top of his class, and then as a PhD holder and law lecturer at the same University, I accummulated a decent amount of knowledge around this topic. Secondly, and most importantly, I want to give you a gift: peace of mind. What sort of peace of mind? What I like to call the autopilot.

I want you to write essay introduction, and thus manage to swiftly start writing any law essay, on autopilot. What do I mean by this? I wnat you to feel secure, to feel safe, to feel like you can always have something in your back pocket, something you can rely on to startt writing.

Not that I want you to hurry! The opposite! In every exam I ever sat for, I was the last student to start writing, and I didn't do badly...My advice here is not meant to make you rush, but to ensure that, once you have given the essay prompt/question some proper thought, you can start writing without needing to reinvent the wheel every single time.

Let's get to it. The autopilot I mentioned has an acronym. The acronym is this: PA. By PA, I will be referring to "Paraphrase and Argue. Let us tackle each one in turn.

By Paraphrase, what I mean is the need to paraphrase the question given, or the essay prompt provided. Essentially, what is required here is an explanation, using synonyms and NOT the exact same words given to you, to describe what the question is about. For instance, if the question is "Has EU law irreversibly undermined parlimentary sovereingty?", which could very well have been a Public Law exam question pre-Brexit, a good way to paraphrase it would be as follows. What the question essentially asks is whether the law of the European Union has overly limited, in a way that cannot be undone,. the power of the Westminster Parliament to make or unmake any law whatever.

What have we thus achieved? Why is this formulation better than straight up repeating the wording of the question word-for-word? Well, for one, even a parrot can repeat, but it cannot paraphrasing. Paraprashing requires a certain "digestion" of the question asked. This signals to the marker that you have actually understood rthe question, and does so at the very beginning of the essay. As we said, first impressions matter, and they last. Secondly, paraphrasing helps you explain the question to yourself too, and find possible angles of "attack". Thirdly, it is the easiest and fastest way to start writing your essay on autopilot.

How about the second half of PA? How about "Argue"? What does it mean and why do you need to start your essays by immediately stating your argument?

Let us answer the second question first, before moving on to what arguing entails. You will hear different views on this topic, so here's mine, as shaped by my years in Oxford. A famous law Professor had told us law students, in one of our first seminars, that law essays are "not mystery novels: the reader should not have to wait until the end to find out who the murderer is". This piece of advice stayed with me and I would really like it to stay with you too.

There are numerous reasons why I think this is golden advice. To begin with, stating your argument at the beginning reveals to the reader the direction of your essay. This way, there is no ambiguity about where this essay is goingh. This shows self-confidence, as well as that you have thought this through and understand that, even though the question asked is complicated, you are not on the fence. Moreover, since the reader knows where this is going, they can assess each subsequent sub-argument by viewing it in light of your overarching argument. Instead of wondering why is the student mentioning this at paragraph 5, they can safely assume that you are doing so because it advances your principal line of argument.

If your argument is not clearly stated in the introduction to your essay, you will have two main problems. First, the marker will probably have to read it twice. This is bad news. No, wrong, this is really bad news. The reason why is because the more times you will force the reader to read your essay in order to understand it, the more errors she is likely to spot (plus, the more annoyed she will feel). The second problem is that you will appear to be a student who is not confident enough to defend an argument, even though you have (hopefully) attended the lectures and done the reading for this essay. This is also bad news. By the time of the formative (or summative) assessment, you need to be in a position to hold strong views on the subject at hand. If not, the marker, who is most probably also your course leader (and principal lecturer) will be justified in feeling that their lectures did not benefit you enough. How can you still be on the fence?

This rhetorical question brings me to my next major point. I am not asserting that you need to have all the answers when arguing in favour of a certain position in your essay introduction. I am not maintaining that you need to appear arrogant, or make it seem as if there is only one correct answer to the essay question. No. This would be both incorrect and unwise. It would be incorrect simply because there is almost never one single correct answer to any given essay question. If there was one, this question would not have been chosen (as an essay question, perhaps as a multiple choice one). Therefore, resist the urge to present your view/argument as the only correct one. Secondly, this would be unwise because, by not being diplomatic and just forcefully asserting that your view is the only correct one, you are essentially showing that your essay is not sophisticated enough. If it were, you would be able to be nuanced, accept the good qualities of the opposing side's argument, and then show why your arguments should prevail. This has to be done via your own integration of the opposing view's merits in your own views. So: nuanced yet argumentative beats absolute and overconfident every day of the week. The way forward for you should look like this. Never on the fence, but also never too far away! Be nuanced, diplomatic, clever, but at the same time assertive and convincing!

This brings me to a final point about your choice of words. This is a lesson I learned the hard way during my first year in Oxford as a law student. Never use the words right and wrong about a view you do not endorse. Just don't. Trust me, the marker will appreciate it. Law is a relative "discipline". Apart from outright mistaken assertions. e.g. that the Magna Carta was signed yesterday, all else is probably arguable. By dismissing a view as wrong you are doing yourself a disservice and are not being academic enough. Your go-to words in these scenarios, instead of right and wrong, should be "reasonable" and "unreasonale", "compelling" and "not compelling" etc etc. You are not naive enough to believe that you are going to be the judge of what is right and wrong, but you can certainly judge an assertion as being unreasonable, you can surely discern whether an argument is untenable etc etc. Use words carefully! Careful phrasing will allow you to escape many traps and will certainly help you improve your marks.

**

Can literature teach us anything about how to write an essay introduction? What can we learn from the opening lines of brilliant books?

'Many years later, as he faced the firing squad, Colonel Aureliano Buendía was to remember that distant afternoon when his father took him to discover ice.' [One Hundred Years of Solitude, by Gabriel García Márquez]

'It was the best of times, it was the worst of times, it was the age of wisdom, it was the age of foolishness, it was the epoch of belief, it was the epoch of incredulity, it was the season of Light, it was the season of Darkness, it was the spring of hope, it was the winter of despair, we had everything before us, we had nothing before us, we were all going direct to Heaven, we were all going direct the other way'. [A Tale of Two Cities, by Charles Dickens]

'If I have learned anything in this long life of mine, it is this: in love we find out who we want to be; in war we find out who we are.' [The Nightingale by Kristin Hannah]

What do all of the above have in common? They are the opening lines of great books. Fascinating novels written by brilliant writers, true wordsmiths that treated writing as a sacred craft.

An arresting opening line serves multiple purposes. First, it grabs the reader's attention. Second, it sets the the scene for what will ensue: a good opening line will probably be followed by good prose. Third, it is memorable. Many novels' opening lines have been immortalised and are known even by people that never read the book itself. The opening line of Moby-Dick ("Call me Ishmael.") is a good example.

What can we (lawyers, legal scholars, judges, law students) learn from literature? Well, the list is endless, but let us just focus on opening lines for now. It is common knowledge that, more frequently than not, legal writing can get a bit dry and technical. The writer usually gets straight to the point, using no literary devices to help the reader more easily navigate the detailed material she presents. Analogies are absent, and so are metaphors and allusions. Sometimes we do encounter the odd quote, but this remains the exception.

What literature teaches us, inter alia, is that the benefits of intriguing opening lines transcend writing genres. Good writing is good writing, whether it's literature, advertising, legal essays or court judgments. It is therefore advisable to take the "risk" of relying on them to get readers hooked before driving our point home.

Having mentioned court judgments, it is worth stressing that some brilliant opening lines can be found in judgments. Here are some fine examples:

'In my view, the parties do not need a judge; what they need is a rather stern kindergarten teacher.' Justice E.Morgan of the Ontario Superior Court in Morland-Jones v Taerk, 2014 ONSC 3061.

'I will call her Janet because she has had four surnames already.' Lord Denning in Eves v Eves [1975] EWCA Civ 3.

'Overnight on 29th January 2012 the Defendant, Fatih Ozcan had a dream.' HHJ Gosnell in Kucukkoylu v Ozcan [2014] EWHC 1972 (QB).

And of course, Lord Denning's most famous opening line: 'It happened on April 19, 1964. It was bluebell time in Kent.' Lord Denning in Hinz v Berry [1970] 2 QB 40.

The link between great literature and good legal writing is there for us to explore. Who knows? At the end of the day we might come to conclude that 'it was love at first sight', to use the opening line from Joseph Heller's bestseller "Catch-22".

CHAPTER 5

How to Argue

How exactly do you argue? How do you craft an argument? Well, first, you need to focus on the subject at hand. What is the essay about? Reforming tort law? Examining the impact of the European Convention of Human Rights on the right to privacy? Assessing the limits of the royal prerogative? You need to first focus on the subject, so that you can understand it.

Then, what exactly are you being asked to do? Critically evaluate? Assess? Are you given an essay prompt and asked to "discuss"? Depending on what you are being asked to do, you change your approach. Still, to be honest, there is not a huuuge amount of difference between these prompts. At the end of the day, whatever essay you are being asked to produce, you need to be "critical". You also need to be argumentative. No summative assessment at a top Uni will ask you to simply describe something. Therefore, always be ready to produce top quality stuff, whatever the prompt.

Let's now come to the (in)famous Oxonian "Discuss." that comes after long and cryptic essay prompts. Here, the first step is to read the quote, spot the keywords and then find your angles of attack.

Not all words are created equal. Some are more "equal" than others. You need to spot them in the essay prompt and dissect them by carefully defining them. Your definition will also allow you to define (and cleverly limit) the scope of your essay. For instance, in a prompt about effective judidical protection, you can define the latter by limiting it to domestic and not international courts, and then say that "effectiveness" will be approached from the perspective of the citizens and not the State. This is a reasonable way to both define and limit the scope of the essay.

Still, the best piece of advice I have given my students is about the assumptions underlying an essay question or an essay prompt. Hundreds of my student have repeatedly told me how this piece of advice singlehandedly revolutionised the way they approached essay writing and made their marks skyrocket.

The recipe is simple. Every essay question you have ever encountered rested upon a set of (implicit) assumptions. For instance, if the question is "To what degree does the HRA 1998 reflect the content of the ECHR?", this assumes that it does reflect the content, and simply asks to what a degree. Similarly, a question on "How has the Francovich principle of state liability for the breach of EU law affected the effectiveness of EU law implementation?" makes various assumptions. One, that there is such a coherent principle in the ECJ's case law. Two, that this principle has affected, to a certain extent, EU law effectiveness, and you are being asked to merely ascertain the how and not the if. Third, that EU law effectiveness is an EU law principle which has something to do with EU law implementation.

Great! So, now you know what the assumptions are. What are you to do with this knowledge? First, you need to point them out! You need to show the marker that you did not shift straight into "answer mode", but you tried to look behind the question and unpack its hidden and implicit assumptions. This shows that you are meticulous and you paid a lot of attention to the question. Very few, if any, of your fellow examinees will have done this. Take advantage of it and stand out!

Second, you need to engage with these assumptions. Don't just point them out, tell the reader what you think about them! Are they reasonable? Do they make sense? Are they self-evident? If yes, then explicitly endorse them. Say you agree, you accept them, and that's the only reason why you are now going to jump into answering the question exactly as it was posed. However, more often than not, there will be some sort of controversy in these assumptions. One or more of them will not be self-evident, and might even be highly contested. Perfect! Now you have found your first target! Attack it with all your might. Remember: you have found a target that most, if not all, of your fellow examinees have missed! Merely by attacking it after you identified it, you are gaining marks. You start your essay writing being one step ahead of everyone from the very beginning.

Then, depending on whether the assumption you identified is reasonable or not, the way forward can take various directions. One of the bet scenarios for you is that the assumption is unreasonable and not easily defensible. This means your attack will be successful. With a series of solid arguments, backed up by footnotes citing primary and secondary sources, the assumption will collapse. This means that you have started off with a victory, since you are now going to be able to demonstrate that there is a single most persuasive answer to the essay question,and the reason is that one of its assumptions is flawed, and therefore the only real answer lies with your arguments. Attacking assumptions can be very rewarding of they colapse. Still, even if they don't, even if they prove sturdy and, after scrutinising them, you conclude that they are valid assumptions, you will be one of the select few who took the time to wrestle with the assumptions before concluding that they actually hold water. Having done your "background check", you can now proceed rto answer the actual question.

Long story short: in your essay introduction, always paraphrase and argue, always identify the keywords and always look for implicit assumptions and try to challenged them!

* * *

It is now worth discussing how a law student can work towards forming her own legal opinion on a particular legal issue or debate.

I have noticed that many law students, especially first-year undergrads, struggle with this. They frequently ask me and their other course leaders: "Professor So-and-so has said everything there is to be said, how do I go beyond that?". Or: "this Supreme Court ruling is very persuasive, how could anyone argue against it?" etc etc.

If this sounds like you, then please know it is completely normal to feel this way; it's happening for a reason. You have just entered a brave new world (the study of law) and you find yourselves reading articles and judgments written by experts who have spent decades honing their skills. Of course everything sounds persuasive and every single line of argumentation seems … water-tight!

However, as we have analysed before, in matters of legal argumentation, there is no single, objective, overarching truth. Law is a grey area par excellence. Therefore, there is always room for your … "grey" views too!

The main reason why you find it hard to form your own legal opinion on, say, whether capital punishment should be legal, or on whether e.g. the Sovereignty of the Westminster Parliament was eroded by the UK's participation in the EU, is that you think you are being asked for an opinion that is … bullet-proof. But this is not the case!

When you are asked to answer an essay question, your law lecturer is not asking you to come up with the "perfect" argument, nor to "defeat" all of the arguments of Lord Whomever; just to contribute to the debate in a way that is logical, reasonable and well-researched. That's it!

In other words, your law lecturer is not scouring your essay for a killer argument; instead, she is interested in hearing YOUR argument, i.e. your own unique blend of hypotheses, reasoning, selection of primary and secondary sources, all amalgamated by your unique writing style.

So, to conclude: forming your own legal opinion is tough, but not as daunting as many of you seem to think. Keep calm and keep writing!

* * *

A frequent mistake encountered in the law essays of (mainly) first-year law students is that they are overly descriptive.

Please allow me to elaborate. Having recently graduated high school, some first year law students are slow to adapt to the writing style required by their course leaders. More specifically, in many high schools, students are primarily asked to produce descriptive essays, where they demonstrate their understanding of both sides of a given debate and accurately reproduce the main points.

As a law student, this skill set is necessary, but not sufficient. Essay questions invite you to take a stand on the question asked and critically assess the prompt/quote given. A wholly descriptive account will not cut the mustard.

Of course, this is a difficult exercise and students have trouble adapting swiftly. This is understandable. You should not be discouraged by essay feedback criticising your (perhaps overly) descriptive essays. You should instead try to comprehend that not taking a stand is as risky as arguing in favour of the solution you find more convincing.

Remember: in matters of legal argumentation, there is no single, objective, overarching truth. No argument should ever be dismissed or endorsed without some critical examination. Arguments that are logically coherent cannot be "right" or "wrong"; they can only be "convincing", "reasonable", or the opposite.

When drafting a law essay, you should leave behind the manichaeistic assessment of the world and embrace the fact that most law "exists" in a grey area. This is an area in which you will gradually start feeling more and more comfortable, finally free to develop your own thoughts and arguments. Embrace this newfound freedom and the accompanying responsibility. This is your time to be heard.

***

"Does it matter what a judge had for breakfast?"

It's eye-catching, isn't it?

It's hard not to do a double-take when encountering such a question. It's even harder not to take a stab at an answer, even subconsciously.

So, why have I chosen this question as an example?

Firstly, to get your attention – this probably worked, since you are reading this sentence.

Secondly, and more importantly, to use it as an example of how to answer open-ended essay questions.

Please keep in mind that the exact same question was included in the general paper of the 2014 All Souls Examination Fellowship. Thought to be "the hardest exam in the world", according to the Guardian, this exam has been … tormenting the brightest Oxford graduates for almost a century now.

So, how would one go about answering this question?

To begin with, the actual answer (yes or no, it matters or it doesn't) is of no real significance, in the sense that your final answer per se doesn't tell the examiner much about your analytical ability and your clarity of thought and expression. What matters is how you answer the question, i.e. how you break it down, identify its keywords, unravel its assumptions and construct a compelling argument.

So, here is the question again: does it matter what a judge had for breakfast?

Firstly, a bit of context. It is noteworthy that this is not a normative question. There is no "should it matter", but simply "does it matter". It is more of a descriptive/evaluative question. This question is actually based on an old adage that "justice is what the judge had for breakfast", used mostly as a way of criticizing the legal realists' school of thought. According to this school, the quality of judicial decision-making does not depend heavily on legal factors (case law, knowledge of the law, proper representation), but on non-legal factors, such as…judges' postprandial mood.

Regardless of whether this is accurate or not, one must endeavour to answer it without any recourse to relevant research you might be unaware of (and yes, it exists), since, for the purposes of this exercise we are assuming that this is a closed-book exam and we are more interested in your way of arguing rather than your arguments per se.

So, what are the keywords in the essay question? I would assert that there are three: "matter", "judge", and "breakfast". The keywords need to be defined by the examinee, in a reasonable manner. For instance, "does it matter" could be translated into "does it have an impact on judicial decision making". A "judge" can reasonably limited to "normal" judges, i.e. members of the judiciary in a State, arbitrators and other individuals passing judgment being excluded. Finally, "breakfast" isn't literally… breakfast but could (obviously) be lunch, if we are referring to an afternoon court session, and anything else that is non-legal and could arguably affect a judge's disposition before entering the courtroom (e.g. a car accident, heavy traffic, arguing with their spouse etc.).

Moving on, following the essay-writing strategy I have detailed in my free PDF guide (you can get it by simply subscribing to this blog), you need to Paraphrase and Argue (PA). Paraphrase what? The question! How do you do that? By using synonyms to restate the question and show the reader you comprehend its meaning. A good attempt to paraphrase "does it matter what a judge had for breakfast?" could be: "The essay question invites us to consider whether non-legal factors such as postprandial mood affect a judge's decision-making ability and/or the quality of her decisions".

Then, you need to state your essay thesis. For instance, assuming you think it does matter, you can say: "In this essay, it is asserted that this does, in fact, matter".

Paraphrase and Argue. That's it. This is all you need for a succinct and complete introduction. The examiner/reader now knows two key things: she is going to read an essay that is not off topic (since you have shown that you have understood the question) and she knows where the essay is going, i.e. that you will be arguing in a particular direction.

There is a piece of advice that I received as a student in Oxford and which I will never forget: essays are not mystery novels! We don't want to have to wait till the end to find out what's going on. You are not Agatha Christie (although that would be cool, right?). State your argument from the beginning, so that the reader knows where this is going and can more easily follow…the plot.

Then, what is left is the main body of your essay and the conclusion. The purpose of your essay's main body is to justify and substantiate the claim you made in your introduction. Why is it that you have taken this particular approach? What primary and secondary sources are you engaging with in order to make your case?

As for the conclusion, its purpose is to come full circle and complete what the introduction started. For instance, you can say: in this essay, it has been argued that non-legal factors such as postprandial mood do affect a judge's decision-making ability and/or the quality of her decisions.

That's it! Click submit and…enjoy your First Class mark ☺

CHAPTER **6**

The Main Body of the Essay

Your introduction has been written. You followed all of my instructions and you have now produced an excellent introduction (hopefully). What now? I am afraid your job is not over... The real part starts now!

What is the purpose of the main body of your essay? It is simple. You need to fulfill the promise you gave the reader in your introduction. You need to actually "prove", through an array of weel-researched and well-presented primary and secondary sources, that your argument must carry the day. You asserted, in your essay introduction, that one particular answer is the most suitable answer to the essay question. Alternatively, you submitted that a particular interpretation of the essay prompt/quote, or dissection thereof, was the best way forward. Why is that? Now is the time to demonstrate why.

SUBCHAPTER A – A few general pointers

Here are some pointers to help you navigate the main (and longest) part of your essay. First, please make sure to cite as many primary and secondary sources as possible. They are the reason why your essay will be persuasive. Dont' merely tell us what you think. Tell us who else agrees, with whom you disagree, and why. This is academia. It's not "just because", but it's an assertion for a reason. This shows that you know that your ideas don't exist in a vacuum, that others have said similar or contrary things and that, most importantly, you have done the reading! This is how you know everyone's views.

A key point: never just cite someone's opinion. Always ENGAGE with their opinion too, so that the reader can know where you stand. It is not enough to merely quote what Professor X or Professor Y said. It is necessary, but not sufficient. Anyone can do this. More importantly, your marker/professor knows what these professors have written. What they don't know, but wish to find out through your essay, is what YOU think about what they have written. Do you agree? Do you disagree? You need to let the reader know!

Still, how do you let the reader know without major digressions and without spending too many words? You do not have the time, nor the words (due to word limits), to spend on e.g. refuting the argument of every single author you cite. Sure, you can do this with the major authors/academics/judges in this area of law, but not with all of them! How do you overcome this obstacle?

The answer is easy: you will use adverbs. What do I mean? Instead of writing "as Craig argues" you will write "as Craig convincigly argues". Instead of saying "as noted by Alison Young", you will say "as aptly noted by Alison Young. This shows the reader where you stand. Now, they have two pieces of information instead of just one. First, they know that you actually delved into secondary sources and have navigated the relevant academic literature. Second, they know you have not only understood it, since you selected a quote from said source which "fits" the essay, but you also have an opinion about it. In other words, you are diligent enough to do your homework and intelligent enough to engage with the top experts in the area. You have academic courage and are not afraid to express it! This brings me to my next point.

As I stressed in the chapter about essay introductions, you should never ever be on the fence. Let me once again repeat why. You think it is risky to adopt a position and put forward an argument. You feel safer on the fence. You actually believe that both positions are equally persuasive and you do not feel comfortable picking a side. You do not wish to take a risk.

Well, guess what? Not picking a side is not a luxury you can afford, and there is nothing riskier than being on the fence. Choose! Lawyers and law students need to be able to pick a side, judges cannot afford to sit on the fence. Law is not philosophy, where endless discussions are allowed to lead to nowhere (and rightly so). Law is philosophy forced to take a stand. Thus, you need to choose! You need to have an argument, and you need to state it in your essay introduction.

OK, but what does this have to do with the main body of the essay? Well, I have three words for you, which I would like you to memorise: "single argumentative thread". This should be your north star. For every essay, you need to have a signle argumentative thread, i.e. a line of argument that starts from the introduction, is followed through in the main body, and comes full circle in your conclusion.

What this means is that you must not lose the thread! Every single sentence in your essay needs to advance your main argument. For every single sentence you add to your essay, you need to ask yourself two questions. One, is this added sentence absolutely necessary? Two, does it advance the argument I promised to support in my essay introduction? If the answer is yes to both questions, then you should proceed. If you got a "no", scrap the sentence; don't add it.

I cannot stress the importance of the single argumentative thread enough. It helps you stay on target and, more importantlty, it guides your reader towards the finale you had promised them. The reader/marker/professor should never feel lost! They should never be left wondering "why am I reading this paragraph now about the Magna Carta?" or "why is this case being cited?". It should be obvious to them that this article or this case is cited because it advances your argument, either by supporting it, or by you citing it to refute it. Therefore, the single argumentative thread idea means that the reader always knows the direction of your essay and never scratches her head. You cannot fathom how many essays violate this rule. The writing is confusing and many paragraphs are either out of place or completely irrelevant and unnecessary. This frustrates the reader and costs you marks. Do not do it! Keep close to your heart these three golden words: single argumentative thread!

Moving on, let us now discuss the appropriate balance between primary and secondary sources in the main body of your essay. By way of reminder, a primary source is legislation and case law, while secondary source is a piece of academic literature, e.g. a book or a journal article. What should the balance be between the two? Well, I will give you the typical lawyer's answer: it depends. Here comes the second most important question: what does it depend on? It depends on the question. If you get a question that is purely or pirncipally theoretical, it is OK to scew the balance 80-20 in favour of secondary sources. For instance, if the question is about the justification underlying criminal punishment, you will have to rely on theoretical debates more. Same if the question is about the role that the rule of law has to play as a limitation to parliamentary sovereignty. However, even here, it should not be 100-0. If you cannot find any legislation or case to cite at all, then just find one that makes a point similar to the one you are trying to make. As a last resort, use real life examples to show what you wish to demonstrate.

Now, if the question is more practical, or revolves around a passage taken from a case or a section from a piece of legislation, your focus should be much more practical, without ignoring the theoretical angles. You should mention all relevant case law and legislation. You should delve into the facts of each case and understand its difference with other cases. You should check whether you can extrapolate from the facts of the key case involved and apply them to other factual scenarios. Still, you always need secondary sources! The key piece here is obviously case comments in top academic journals. Google them or find them through the online system of your university library. Apart from Google per se, also use the Google Scholar search; it is quite useful.

So, how do you use case comments? Well, first, you read them in order to understand the "history" behind a seminal case. How did it change or add to previous case law? Second, you read it to understand its significance. Third, you read it to comprehend the author's view about this case. Do they think it was persuasive and well-written? Or not? If not, why not? Do you agree with their reservations?

And now, most importantly, WHAT DO YOU THINK about their assessment? Was it fair? Was the criticism merited? Perhaps the opposite happened... Did they, instead of writing a case comment, put together a hagiography of the judges involved? Have they praised the rationale so much that they have covered up all the flaws that you see? That's excellent! You can now use them to attack the case, while at the same time exposing the shortcomings of their case comment.

Everything you read is ammunition. Let me repeat this. Everything you read is ammunition. Use it!

SUBCHAPTER 2 – No historical background is necessary in 90% of essays

I hate it when essays start with a historical analysis of everything that has happened in this area of law since the middle ages. Some even go back to Ancient Greece and then Ancient Rome. Stop it! Your attempt to show off, coupled with your attempt to reach the word count, is messing up your essays. You do not need to do this! It is very rare that it will actually be necessary for you to go back to the Middle Ages and devote two entire paragraphs on what the legal system looked like back then. It is also very rarely necessary to explain that contract law has been crucial in all societies since Ancient Mesopotamia! So, key takeaway: do not discuss any historical data unless it is absolutely necessary and it somehow answers the question directly or makes your argument more persuasive!

SUBCHAPTER 3 – Forget long paragraphs

One of the sins I was guilty of myself, as a newcomer in Oxford, was writing in suuuper long sentences and paragraphs. In fact, sometimes my sentences would four or five lines long, and my paragraphs would cover most of the page! It was a nightmare for the reader but I did not know better. I think this is a sin that continental students commit more than UK students, but it needs to be stressed regardless.

Try to remember a few rules. Number 1: your reader/marker/professor is already very tired. She has read dozens of essays on the same topic and will read many more. Avoid making her life harder by having her go back to the beginning of your sentnece just to remember what the verb or the subject was! You need to help her understand you, not torture her (disregard any possible animosity you might have against her; just kidding!). Number 2: Never write a sentence that is more than three lines long! Break it into two or more sentences, thus keeping it short and sweet. Number 3: Try to use more simple sentneces and fewer complex sentences. For example, you could say: Tort law changed a lot after the Roy case, which was decided in 1976, during a period of unrest, the cause of which was civil war. However, this is overly complicated for no reason. Instead of drafting it this way, kindly consider ephrasing to make it easier to read and digest. A good example would be this: Tort law changed drastically after the Roy case, a which was decided in 1976. This was a period of unrest, the cause of which was civil war.

All of the above is obviously made up, but I just wanted to show how to break a sentence into more, smaller sentences. It is very easy and good help you improve your marks in no time.

This brings me to a broader point. If you ever mark the exam scripts or summative assessments of undergraduate students, even at top universities,you will be shocked by rthe sheer number of grammatical and syntactical errors. Not only do native English speakers make serious mistakes, they keep making them throughout their three or four years of study. Therefore, by simply NOT making such errors, you are standing out from a large majority of the crowd.

So, key takeaways from this section. First, respect your reader and value their time and effort. Their job is hard enough, don't make it harder. They will reward you for it. second, break your sentences into shorter sentences, and your paragraphs into more paragraphs. Your essay will be easier to read and understand. Third, proofread your essays before submitting! This way you will avoid making grammatical and syntactical errors and thus improve your overall marks.

SUBCHAPTER 4 - The art of footnotes

Footnotes can be boring. Writing them even more than reading them. Still, they form the backbone of a good law essay, let alone of a good law article or book.

What is their purpose? Firstly, they are there for you to "park" your citations. The hospitable bosom of these small footnotes will happily accept anything from R v Brown to Factortame and Francovich. It will groan if you only cite primary sources (statutes, case law etc.), and it will scowl if you only cite secondary sources (books, articles etc.). Thus, a balanced mix is imperative.

Secondly, footnotes are there for you to laconically go on an excursus. You should not fill them with paragraphs upon paragraphs of comments in a vain effort to circumvent the word count for your essay, given that footnotes do not usually count. No. You must resist this urge. Footnotes are there for you to clarify your arguments or further explain certain points that would break the flow of your essay and/or are not important enough to make it to the body of your essay . Use them for this reason and this reason alone.

Thirdly, footnotes are important for law students' essays because they are very frequently relied upon by law professors s a first indication of the quality of a law essay (oh yes). This might come as a surprise to some of you but, in my experience and opinion, footnotes are one of the most accurate ways of forming an initial view on the quality of a student's law essay. This is so for multiple reasons. Firstly, your footnotes reveal the breadth of your reading and the depth of your research. Secondly, it shows your law lecturer whether you have actually read the reading assigned by them in the reading list, thus illustrating that you can follow instructions and that you have gone through the reading list diligently. Thirdly, the footnotes will demonstrate to what an extent you have avoided repetition; if all the reader sees is "ibid", "ibid" and… "ibid", then the variety of your sources is most probably not ideal.

To sum up, your footnotes say more about your work than you may have previously imagined. Therefore, it is worth reassessing your strategy and paying more attention to the neglected art of footnoting.

SUBCHAPTER 5 – Read the Actual Cases

For many law students, actually reading the cases listed on their reading list in their entirety resembles a Herculean task.

First, there seems to be no time. Second, there is no point: they can find good (?) summaries online, sometimes even on Wikipedia! Why bother?

There are many answers to this rhetorical question. Firstly, most summaries you will find online are neither good not accurate. Secondly, we (law professors/lecturers) can instantly understand whether you've actually read the case or whether you are simply regurgitating the summary we have just read in many other students' essays. Thirdly, and most importantly, it's very bad practice not to read cases and only rely on summaries, either found online or in textbooks.

Why? There are several reasons, but I will only focus on two:

A) Court cases form the "bricks" of the legal discipline, both in common and in civil law systems. They are the primary material on which, together with statutes, the legal edifice is built. Having only a superficial knowledge of them will make it harder for you to understand the "why" and "how" of the law, while also exposing your flanks to counterarguments you never expected.

B) If you were a historian, would you expect to get away with not reading the actual primary sources, e.g. the account of a battle in the memoirs of a general, and only read the general description of that same battle by a historian writing 200 years later? Isn't this similar to only reading the textbook account of a case instead of the actual case itself? Do you see the main problem here? The problem is that you are not learning about the actual case, you're just reading someone's else views about said case, which might very well be different to the one you would have formed. Perhaps, in your view, the key facts/paragraphs/dicta and takeaways would have been different. How can you know if you don't read the case yourself?

So, let me come full circle and thus conclude this section the way I advise you to conclude your essays: Read the Actual Cases!

CHAPTER **7**

Essay Conclusions

Every drink, every meal, every memory that you have is remembered by the aftertaste it left you. If it was good, you remember it as even better. If it was bad, you remember it as even worse. Impressions matter, and final impressions matter even more!

Therefore, it is crucial that your conclusion pithy, laconic and to the point. The role of the conclusion is to close the circle you opened in your essay's introduction. Your introdction included a promise to the reader: "in this essay it will be asserted that...". In your conclusion, you need to remind the reader that you actually fulfilled said promise. How do you do this?

Well, an easy nadswift way to do this is to rephrase the introduction, but in past tense now. In the intro you said: it will be asserted. Here, in the conclusion, you will start by writig: In this essay, it has been submitted that...etc. This way, you show the reader that you never forgot what you had set out to "prove", and you demonstrate the end of your single argumentative thread. It began in the intro, it unravelled and blossomed in the main body, and now it comes to an end. The perfect mark of a structured and "disciplined" essay!

Now, discussing what you should not do in your essay's conclusion is equally crucial! Here are some pointers. First, you should never ever ever ever introduce new arguments in your conclusion! Never. The conclusion has to represent a recap of your major points, without new points appearing out of nowhere. You might wonder: who does this? I have done rthis, you have done this, almost everyone does, but you don't always understand it! That's the problem. For instance, you might say: "therefore, the assertion in the essay prompt needs to be rejected because XYZ" without realising that after the word "because" you added something either had not mentioned in the essay or had mentioned it differently and thus now appears rather novel. Don't do it! delete this sentence and save yourself a few precious marks.

I know what you are thinking. "But I almos always run out of time and write the conclusion last so it is always rather hastily written why do you expect so much of me?" Answer: I ask for almost nothing! cJust summarise and conclude! You can be as laconic as you like! This is the bare minimum.

Of course, for those of you that always seek something more, I've got you covered... In my view, if you can, make your conclusion memorable, you are already a victor.

If you can make the ending memorable, you have won!

This principle applies to movies, books, music score and – yes – law essays. There are numerous reasons why your essay's conclusion has to be well drafted. Firstly, it is the last impression the reader receives from your essay, the final taste. Make it a sweet one.

Secondly, frequently the reader, especially if they are marking your essay, might take a quick look at your conclusion right after they read your introduction. This serves a dual purpose. One, this way they verify that what you "promised" in the introduction actually materialised in the conclusion. Two, this way they can be sure that the conclusion is pithy and on point.

The third reason why it is important for your conclusion to be memorable is that it allows you to illustrate that you understand the basic rule of conclusions, which is: do not add new information and make new arguments in the conclusion! The conclusion is only there for you to laconically summarise the key points of your essay and "close the loop" of your essay, i.e. make it come full circle. The conclusion is where you demonstrate that you compellingly argued what you had set out to argue.

No more, no less.

In conclusion, make your conclusion memorable!

CHAPTER 8

(Re)writing like Hemingway

His prose was legendary. Few writers could go toe-to-toe with a litterateur like Hemingway:

"But man is not made for defeat... A man can be destroyed but not defeated."

"There is nothing else than now. There is neither yesterday, certainly, nor is there any tomorrow. How old must you be before you know that?"

"– How did you go bankrupt? – Two ways. Gradually, then suddenly."

"All my life I've looked at words as though I were seeing them for the first time."

"As you get older it is harder to have heroes, but it is sort of necessary."

"Any man's life, told truly, is a novel..."

"Cowards die a thousand deaths, but the brave only die once."

However, even Hemingway found writing to be rather arduous: *"There is nothing to writing. All you do is sit down at a typewriter and bleed."*

Today, we are going to revisit some of his advice or writing, rewriting and getting started. The excerpts below come from the book "Ernest Hemingway on Writing".

When Hemingway got stuck, he would repeat these dicta to

himself: *"Do not worry. You have always written before and you will write now. All you have to do is write one true sentence. Write the truest sentence that you know." So finally I would write one true sentence, and then go on from there. It was easy then because there was always one true sentence that I knew or had seen or had heard someone say."*

In order to keep the creative juice flowing, Hemingway advised that you need to *"write until you come to a place where you still have your juice and know what will happen next and you stop and try to live through until the next day when you hit it again. You have started at six in the morning, say, and may go on until noon or be through before that. When you stop you are as empty, and at the same time never empty but filling, as when you have made love to someone you love. Nothing can hurt you, nothing can happen, nothing means anything until the next day when you do it again. It is the wait until the next day that is hard to get through."*

When it came to selecting words, the author should bid…farewell to adjectives, rather than arms: *'[Ezra was]… the man who had taught me to distrust adjectives as I would later learn to distrust certain people in certain situations…'*

When asked how much rewriting he did, his reply was: *"It depends. I rewrote the ending to Farewell to Arms, the last page of it, thirty-nine times before I was satisfied."* When asked what took him so long, he laconically retorted: *"Getting the words right".*

If even a literary giant like Hemingway had trouble writing, mere mortals should not be surprised when hitting a roadblock. All we need to remember is his last piece of advice: *"Every day is a new day. It is better to be lucky. But I would rather be exact. Then when luck comes you are ready."*

CHAPTER 9

Revision Strategy

Sometimes, students ask for advice in relation to what they should do during the Christmas/Easter/summer break. They seem to be anxious about the material they did not manage to cover before the term/year ended, while also fretting about the upcoming mock exams/collections/summative assessments.

A few pieces of advice are, perhaps, in order. Feel free to take them with a pinch of salt and keep in mind that each person's situation is unique:

a) Get some rest. This should be your first priority. Avoid burnout at all costs, since the physical and psychological repercussions will be severe, and it will only impede your academic ambitions. Make sure that, for a good few days, you do absolutely nothing study-related.

b) Reread all the written work you submitted during the term, both formative and summative.

c) Carefully peruse the comments your course leader provided in relation to the aforementioned written work. Then write them all down in a new document and divide them into categories (e.g. comments related to lack academic citations/unclear essay structure/overly descriptive style of writing).

This is now the document you will use as a checklist, i.e. as a document that you will go through before submitting any new written work, in order to ensure that you avoid making the same mistakes.

d) Double down on your strengths. Sometimes, students feel that they are very close to getting a distinction in, say, Contract Law, and they think it wise to "relax" and now only focus on, say, Public Law, which is not their strongest suit. In my view, this strategy is misguided, and is an almost surefire way of not getting any excellent marks at all. The best strategy is to double down on your strengths, keep improving in the course that you are already good at and try to ensure you get a first class mark in them. Don't neglect the other courses, but please don't grow complacent either. In life or in law, when you have an advantage, you need to press it, not abandon it.

That's my (laconic) advice on revision. Hope it helps!

CHAPTER 10
Comparison is the thief of joy

You know the old adage: comparison is the thief of joy. It is true. If you only focus on what you possess, and cherish it, you will be happy. But if you keep comparing your car with the neighbour's car, your weight with the weight of people on instagram and your bank balance with Elon Musk's, you are bound to be miserable.

Don't make the same mistake in relation to academic progress and academic performance. Your only point of reference needs to be yourself yesterday, not other students! Don't be sad because in your last essay you got a 68 while Hannah got 69. This makes no sense. You can be a bit disappointed if you got a 68 this week while last week you got 71, since this means you made no progress. Yes, this does make sense. Anything else is pointless and leads to envy and thus to feelings of inadequacy. You do you. Listen to the tutor's feedback, take it seriously and try to improve, but do not compare yourself to other students. The point about feedback leads me to the next chapter.

CHAPTER 11

Academic feedback and how to receive it

We are usually not upset by a bad mark on its own. We have all been there. What does upset us, however, is when we do not understand "why" exactly we got this mark. We protest against this kind of injustice and we rightly seek to understand why. Unfortunately, I must admit that some students are right. On many occasions, academic feedback is either overly laconic, cryptic or outright non-existent! Tutors and markers at many universities need to up their game and provide more feedback, both because students deserve to know and because this will make markers mark in a abetter way.

So, some principles of academic feedback. First, it has to be as precise as possible. You cannot tell a student to "dig deeper". No! That's sloppuy and lazy. What you should instead do is say "I think your analysis would benefit from a closer look at the 1993 edited volume by so and so and by incorporating recent case law, especially this and that case etc.". Do you see how this is much more precise, helpful and to the point? It is not an abstract exhortation to just "study more", "dig deeper" or anything of this sort. It is actionable advice! So this is how feedback should be given, i.e. by providing specific advice and not abstract criticism. The latter is not helpful; in fact, it is frustrating and counterproductive.

Now, let us zoom towards the student. How should you receive feedback? Should you feel depressed whnever there is even a slither of criticism? Should you panic if it's not full of praise? Of course not! Mark my words: your best performance will alaways come after a period of disappointment. Only once someone has criticised you will you wake up and realise there is more left in the tank. Cherish these moments; they sting, but they are the start of new eras.

Let me pause and share a personal story, since otherwise all this might appear to be overly abstract and theoretical. After completing my undegraduate studies at the Athens Law School, I was admitted to the famous Magister Juris programme of the Oxford University Law School. This is a MAster of Laws, i.e. an LLM, but it's called MJur in Oxford (or BCL if you have a common law undergrad degree). It is extremely competitive, both to gain admission and to do well. The top performers from all universities in the world apply and only the best get in. Therefore, you can imagine that it is an academic lion pit. Almost everyone there seems smarter than you and seems to be working twice as hard. This literally pushes you to your limits. I gained twelve kilos in ten months, studying as much as I could, and practising the principles I am explaining in this book. In the end, I graduated top of my class (Valedictorian) in 2013, thus receiving the Clifford Chance Prize for the Best Overall Performance in the MJur. But this is a story for another day, or another chapter.

One of the episodes that stuck with me, out of the many of that eventful MJur year, was the following. I had just finished a tutorial session with one of the best Oxford law professors (then a young tutor), when he pulled me aside and asked to talk to me in private. You might laugh, but I actually thought he was going to congratulate me, since my tutorial essay had been marked as "excellent" by him. We were also pretty close to exams, so perhaps he wanted to wish me lukc? Well, at least that's what I thought.

Instead of all the above, he actually warned me that I was getting complacent. I was shocked. He said that I keep hovering around 70-71% (a Distinction but still only just) and this means that I might not do as well in the upcoming exams. He warned me I was getting too comfortable and I was not improving. This was really upseting. Not because it was not true. It certainly was! But because it was not what I was expecting.

He also said something else. This is a bit different, but I'll share it here because it shows the importance of knowing your students. This tutor knew that I was more competitive than average, i.e. that competition with other students made me better, not worse. This point is key. Had he said to another student what he told me, it would have backfired. So, getting to know your students is a must, since what might motivate a competitive spirit might completely paralyse someone else.

So, he told me that the silent student in the tutorial session with me (plus another student) had submitted an essay that got a 75%! This is a crazy mark. Student who obtain such marks in the actual exam usually get the award for the best paper, and also get a Prize. So, my jaw dropped. But IO was even more flabbergasted to find out that this student had also previously submitted, in past tutorials, three more essas that received similarly excellent marks! This was really a shock to my system. How could I have been so complacent? So naive? I was fully satisfied with my academic performance, driving on autopilot. I wasn't going anywhere and I was floating on air, while the other student was (humbly and silently) just demolishing all of us! I had to do better.

I never found out if my tutor was telling me the truth. I am 80% sure he was. In any case, I have now realised this is immaterial. He did it because he knew me well, we had a strong bond, he believed in me, and he wanrted me to improve. And it worked. When I secured the top prize in my year's cohort,he was the first professor I emailed. He was not surprised....

So: take feedback seriously. Leverage it to your advantage. Don't ignore it; and certainly don't take it personally.

CHAPTER 12

Managing Expectations

How do you deal with the expectations of others in relation to your academic performance? How do you manage them? Your parents, your siblings, your friends. They all expect something of you. They might not admit it, but they do. It might not be good, mind you! It might be mediocre, or even bad. Their exopectations might be super high or super low. In any case, they exist, and you probably feel a need to live up to thrm.

Listen to me: they cannot, and should not, affect your performance, as long as you stick to the script. Think of it in the following terms. You are taking a penalty; you are a footbhall player. Better still, you are a young Lionel Messi. People expect certain things from you. First, your parents: they raised you, allowed you to chase your dreams, sacrificed for you, put food on the table... Now aht? They expect you to score, right? Yes, theydo.

Secondly, your coach. He started you. Believes in you, gave you a spot. Now, you need to score!

Third, your teammates. They trust you. Their career and how many trophies they will life depends on you too. Their expectations feel heavy on your shoulders.

Finally, your competitors! The opposing team. They are people too and they feel the same way you feel. They expect things from you, they have trained for you, they are ready for you.

How does all of this make you feel? Well, obviously, stressed!

You get performance anxiety. You feel the weight of the world on your shoulders. You do not want to disappoint anyone, but you also don't feel 100% self-confident. Others' expectations are making you feel "heavier". The natural lightness of simply performing is gone.

The exact same applies to academic performance. On the day of the exam, or right before you click "submit" for your summative assessment, you feel the weight of others' expectations. Your parents sacrificed so that uyou can study, and now you won't perform? All your friends have graduated and have done well, now you will be the one left behind? Your course leader was couinting on you to excel, how will you look them in the eye?

Well, all of this does not matter. In fact, thinking about them will make you perform much worse. You don't want your hands to tremble, your stomach to ache. You want to simply be present.

So, just think of the worst case scenario and embrace it, and this will probably calm your nerves and help you perform. What is it? Realistically? You are not going to die if you fail Contract law, right? You will have another shot! Your mark will be capped and affected, yes (probably), but you will still get your degree and be able to practice law, right? Your loved ones will continue to have your back, and you will have theirs.

So, please calm your nerves. This moment is not as important as it seems. Don't let many years worth of effort and studying go to waste because you got nervous. Academic performance, like all performance, needs steady hands and a steady heart. Success is not purely intellectual, it's psychological too…

CHAPTER 13

General Essay Writing Advice

* * *

JK Galbraith on Writing

Recipient of the World War II Medal of Freedom. Recipient of the Presidential Medal of Freedom. Harvard Professor of Economics. Adviser to President Kennedy. US Ambassador to India.

JK Galbraith's CV was as impressive as they get. However, our focus today will be on his writing. Galbraith was a prolific writer, publishing almost 50 books and more than a thousand (!) articles in his lifetime.

Like all good writers, he had his own philosophy on writing, a philosophy that might resonate with many of this blog's readers. In my view, his observations are spot on.

His best piece was "Writing, Typing, and Economics"' an essay which appeared in the March 1978 issue of The Atlantic. The following excerpts are worth our attention:

'[I]n the social sciences, much unclear writing is based on unclear or incomplete thought. It is possible with safety to be technically obscure about something you haven't thought out. It is impossible to be wholly clear on something you do not understand.'

"All writers know that on some golden mornings they are touched by the wand — are on intimate terms with poetry and cosmic truth. I have experienced those moments myself. Their lesson is simple: It's a total illusion. And the danger in the illusion is that you will wait for those moments. Such is the horror of having to face the typewriter that you will spend all your time waiting. I am persuaded that most writers, like most shoemakers, are about as good one day as the next (a point which Trollope made), hangovers apart. The difference is the result of euphoria, alcohol, or imagination. The meaning is that one had better go to his or her typewriter every morning and stay there regardless of the seeming result. It will be much the same..."

"There may be inspired writers for whom the first draft is just right. But anyone who is not certifiably a Milton had better assume that the first draft is a very primitive thing. The reason is simple: Writing is difficult work. Ralph Paine, who managed Fortune in my time, used to say that anyone who said writing was easy was either a bad writer or an unregenerate liar. Thinking, as Voltaire avowed, is also a very tedious thing which men — or women — will do anything to avoid. So all first drafts are deeply flawed by the need to combine composition with thought. Each later draft is less demanding in this regard. Hence the writing can be better..."

Apart from being a brilliant academic with a stellar CV, it is obvious that Galbraith had many wise words to share on the process of writing itself. Reading old gems such as his advice above can certainly help our writing improve, but also encourage us to keep moving forward.

Let me close with one of my favourite quotes on writing, this time by Winston Churchill: "If you have an important point to make, don't try to be subtle or clever. Use a pile driver. Hit the point once. Then come back and hit again. Then hit a third time – a tremendous whack."

* * *

'For the things we have to learn before we can do them, we learn by doing them. Men become builders by building and lyre players by playing the lyre.'

Aristotle

Reading books about how to write legal essays is perfectly fine. In fact, if the feedback you get from your tutors is not detailed enough, the best way to improve is to search for advice from any possible source. This book aims to help you in your search, by providing actionable advice based on years of experience.

However, reading about essay writing is not enough. At some point, you need to actually start honing your craft and practice essay writing rigorously and regularly.

It is trite to say that practice makes perfect. It is also, in a sense, wrong. Not every kind of practice makes perfect; only deliberate practice.

Since the famous article written by Ericsson, Krampe, and Tesch-Römer on "The Role of Deliberate Practice in the Acquisition of Expert Performance" in 1993, the concept of deliberate practice has received a lot of attention. It has also been popularised in the Malcolm Gladwell's bestselling book "Outliers".

As summarised in a recent article by Ericsson, laboratory studies of learning showed that performance was increased when participants "attend to the task and exert effort to improve their performance…. The subjects should receive immediate informative feedback and knowledge of results of their performance. The subjects should repeatedly perform the same or similar tasks".

This quasi-definition of "deliberate practice" gives us a lot of food for thought. Essay-writing alone will not help a student improve her performance and her marks. The student also needs to make sure she focuses on three things.

First, pay attention to the task at hand and make an actual, conscious effort to improve. In other words, she needs to think long and hard about what it takes to produce an excellent essay, and not just try to reach the word limit and hit "submit". This is key.

Second, she needs to ask for (and hopefully receive) swift informative feedback from her tutors or course leaders, whether this pertains to a formative or a summative assessment. This way the student will be able to spot and understand her weaknesses and work on them.

Finally, she needs to repeatedly perform the same or similar tasks, i.e. keep practising essay writing! This means that the practice should continue regardless of whether any deadlines are upcoming. Essay writing should become a standalone habit. You cannot ask yourself to suddenly be ready when the submission date comes around if you have not practiced before.

To sum up, deliberate practice is key. Action is necessary. "He who does something at the head of one regiment," Abraham Lincoln reminds us, "will eclipse him who does nothing at the head of a hundred". Make essay-writing a habit, stick to it and the results might amaze you.

* * *

Play Nice but Win!

"Play Nice But Win" is the autobiography (of sorts) by Michael Dell, founder of Dell Technologies. In essence, Dell walks the reader through his journey of revolutionizing the personal computer industry. This digital-age memoir is certainly worth a read in its entirety, but what I would like to focus on is the book's title and the story behind it.

In essence, "play nice but win" is the book's leitmotif. It was the piece of advice that Dell's parents would give him and his siblings when they were about to play sports or participate in other competitive activities.

Both parts are important. First, play nice: in other words play in a way that is fair, considerate, conscientious and respectful. Still, don't forget to win: you're not merely playing to participate and be beaten by others. You are there to play competitively and prevail.

The fact that both parts are possible is, in my view, the key takeaway. The same applies to the endeavours of law students.

It is both possible (and imperative!) to "play nice" as a law student, while also "wining", i.e. outperforming your past self and your fellow students. However, this is not always what happens. Having participated, as a board member, in numerous academic misconduct boards, I have come to experience first-hand the pressure law students feel to "win", and the extremes to which this can lead them.

By way of example, I need only mention flagrant plagiarism (e.g. copy pasting others' work without citing the source), hiring law tutors to write their assignments, or even sabotaging the work of fellow students. We can all agree that such behaviours are totally unacceptable, but I'm sorry to say that they have proliferated since the start of the pandemic, mainly because it has become more difficult to invigilate exams and ensure fairness.

So, to take a page out of Dell's book, please remember: play nice but win. It's possible. And it's the only way to actually experience the full satisfaction of "winning".

* * *

The Hard Thing about Hard Things

One of the best business books I have read is 'The Hard Thing About Hard Things: Building a Business When There Are No Easy Answers' by Ben Horowitz, one of the most successful angel investors in the US.

His book is full of valuable insights, many of which apply to not only startup founders but (surprisingly?) to law students too. Let's have a look.

"There are only two ways for a manager to improve the output of an employee: motivation and training."

The same applies to you when you are…managing yourself and applying yourself to your studies. Remember why you have chosen to focus on a legal career, visualise the future positive outcomes and keep training – namely studying and practicing writing legal essays.

"Spend zero time on what you could have done, and devote all of your time on what you might do."

How you did last year is of no consequence now. You need to start anew. Stop thinking about your GPA and how it is too late for you to improve now (or any other excuse you might be coming up with) and devote all of your time and effort on what you can actually change. The results might surprise you.

"Sometimes an organization doesn't need a solution; it just needs clarity."

I could not agree more – this is spot on. Sometimes clarity IS the solution, because it allows you to properly rephrase the question and, as Charles Kettering had said, "a problem well-stated is half-solved". So, whether you are seeking a solution (i.e. an answer) to a legal essay, a legal problem question or a job interview, ask yourself whether clarity is what you actually benefit you the most.

"The most important lesson in entrepreneurship: Embrace the struggle."

At the end of the day, as they say, the hard thing about hard things is…that they are hard. If you are someone who aims at the top marks and wishes to excel, you must understand that it is not going to be an easy ride. So, decide if it is worth it and start grinding today. Bon courage and best of luck!

* * *

The "nature" of the exam as a discussion

In essence, what is an exam? In my view, it is a discussion. A discussion taking place between you, i.e. your exam script, and your examiner/course leader/lecturer.

Niccolò Machiavelli, in a 1513 letter to his friend Francesco Vettori, wrote the following:

'Once the evening has arrived, I come home and enter my

study. In the entryway I take off my daytime clothing, covered with mud and dirt, and I put on garments that are royal, and suitable for a court. Changed into suitable clothes, I step into the ancient courts of ancient men. Received lovingly by them, I nourish myself on that food that alone is mine, for which I was born. There I am unashamed to talk with them and ask them the reasons for their actions, and they, with their humanity, answer me. For four hours I feel no boredom, I forget all worries, I do not fear poverty, and am not dismayed by death. I give myself to them entirely.'

Machiavelli put on his best clothes when entering his study to read the Greats, i.e. Plato, Aristotle and their peers. Why? Out of respect, because he felt that he was discussing with them when reading their thoughts. You wouldn't converse with Plato in your pyjamas now, would you? It wouldn't be a good idea I think, especially given that Plato was a skilled wrestler; not a person you want to piss off.

More seriously, coming back to my original point about exams: think of them as a discussion. And in this discussion, your goal is to help the reader answer a single question: has this student evolved since the start of this course? Or am I (the examiner) reading a script that could have been written by a student in, say, September? This is important to your examiner. It shows that her teaching and her efforts have had their intended impact and that she is reading the work of a student that has truly taken in all the lessons of their studies.

* * *

Law lecturers frequently encounter a common trend when asking students why they did not perform well in one course, as opposed to other courses.

The answer is this: well, it's just too…boring! Tort law is boring, Public law is boring, Contract law is boring, etc etc..

My answer: there is no such thing as an (inherently) boring course.

A law course is made boring by either the lecturer teaching

it, the method of delivery or the student's preconceptions and preferences. Period.

It is your task, as a student, to identify what is interesting in your law course, and use that to motivate yourself to delve deeper into it. The better you become at it, the less boring it will appear to be.

In reality, anything can be interesting when you think about it long and hard. The power of observation is unfathomable, and can make anything appear intriguing. Even a…sunfish!

So, if you are bored of a law course, take it upon yourself to make it interesting. Observe it closely, study it more, try to link it to everyday life (e.g. tort law and car accidents) and endeavour to think of its effects on society (e.g. the effects of banking and antitrust regulation).

To conclude: do not allow yourself to get trapped in a never-ending excuse about how boring this or that course is. It's up to you to fix it; so do it!

CHAPTER **14**

Guest contribution by Lord Neuberger

It is an honour for me to include a contribution by Lord Neuberger GBS PC HonFRS, President of the UK Supreme Court from 2012 to 2017, in this book.

Lord Neuberger is widely regarded as one of the most prominent and influential English judges. Before being appointed to the UK Supreme Court, he, inter alia, served as High Court Judge in the Chancery Division, Lord of Appeal in Ordinary and Master of the Rolls. He was called to the Bar in 1974, having previously studied chemistry in Oxford.

His contribution below is full of invaluable insights on the fundamentals of legal communication.

LEGAL WRITING

Whether you are a practising lawyer, a law-maker, a legal academic, a judge, or a law student, the two basic principles of legal communication are the same:

(i) Keep it as clear and simple as possible;

(ii) Remember who you are writing for or speaking to.

Like so many fundamental rules in life, these two principles are very often overlooked in practice, even by experienced people, although they seem obvious when one is told them.

Clarity is of the essence of legal communication. However sophisticated the ideas behind it and however complex its aims, any law must be understandable. If you are drafting or laying down the law, it must be clear, so that people can appreciate what is required of them. If you are explaining the law to others, the clearer and simpler you make it, the more likely you are to get your message across. Anyway, lack of clarity or simplicity is a pretty good giveaway that you don't really understand what you are writing or speaking about. This does not mean that you should eschew stylistic elegance, but if it conflicts with clarity, it must yield.

When writing (or speaking) about the law, do not forget that you are communicating with others, rather than addressing yourself. You must remember that you are writing (or speaking) in order to inform, educate or convince other people. You are not writing (or speaking) to yourself. You should therefore think yourself into the mind of your reader or listener. The questions which should constantly be in your mind is: how do I make myself clear to my audience? How do I convince my audience?

CHAPTER 15

Guest contribution by Professor Nick Barber

It is an honour for me to include a contribution by Professor Nick Barber, Professor of Constitutional Law and Theory at the University of Oxford, in this book.

Professor Barber is a Fellow of Trinity College, Oxford and Associate Dean (Research) at the Oxford Law Faculty.

He has lectured extensively on constitutional law and theory in many countries. He has published many papers in these areas, and his book – The Constitutional State – was published in 2011, and has been widely reviewed. His second book, The Principles of Constitutionalism, was published by Oxford University Press in summer 2018. His most recent book, The United Kingdom Constitution: An Introduction was published in the Clarendon Law Series in late 2021. Both The American Journal of Jurisprudence and The Jerusalem Review of Legal Studies have published collections of essays on his work.

He was founder editor of the United Kingdom Constitutional Law Blog, and he was a co-author, with Jeff King and Tom Hickman, of the blog post that sparked the litigation in Miller, a post which first advanced the arguments eventually adopted by the High Court and Supreme Court. Alongside Richard Ekins, he is co-director of The Programme for the Foundations of Law and

Constitutional Government.

Professor Barber's contribution below shares a key secret to effective communication and compelling essay writing, as well as three excellent tips! I am sure you will enjoy reading it.

Essay Writing: One Secret and Three tips

The Secret

There's a simple secret to successful essay writing – indeed, to successful communication in general. It's a secret that's hidden in plain sight, one often spoken, but rarely heard. And it is this: think about your audience.

Effective communication is manipulation. You have an audience who is, let's assume, willing to listen to you, and your task is to make them think and feel what you want them to think and feel. You need to decide where the audience should be at the end of the process and plan how you will get them there. To do this, you need to consider where the audience is starting from, their current beliefs and knowledge, and identify the types of argument and the presentation that will sway them. Above all, you need to put yourself in their place.

To see the truth of this, think about the lectures you've attended: which were the best and which were the worst? The best lecturer identified the information you needed to know, communicated it in a way that helped you understand it, and made the material interesting. You probably left the lecture feeling that the topic was absorbing, you were smart, and the lecturer was a nice person. In contrast, the worst lecturer will have made the material opaque and boring, it will have been hard to see why the lecturer picked the material, and hard to see how anyone could ever find anything interesting to say about it. You probably left the lecture thinking the topic was dull, you didn't get it, and with a vague but definite sense of antipathy towards the lecturer. The first lecturer thought about their audience, the second lecturer (unless they enjoy inflicting pain) did not.

The secret is applicable to everything you write, including law essays. When you're writing a law essay, think about who your audience is and what you want them to think. Normally, you're writing for your tutor or the examiners. You want them, I expect, to come away from reading the essay thinking that you've understood the material, you have something interesting to say, and, indeed, that they like you. To reach this point, put yourself in their position. You know that they know the material, you know that they have read many essays on the topic. So, you need to include enough bare information to show you understand the material, but, as your reader already knows that information thoroughly, you need to show something more. What is going to raise your mark is critical engagement with the material, rather than mere recitation, and, moreover, critical engagement that is clear and easy to read. If you have made it easy for the reader to understand your argument, the reader will warm to you – make it hard, and the reader might well conclude that there is not really an argument there at all. Your tutors and, even more so, your examiners will not be prepared to dig all that deep to unearth your argument.

That is the secret. I have a few tips to help you get your audience where you want them, but these are all just elaborations of the core message: be sensitive towards those who are listening to you or reading your work.

Structure

The first tip is to think hard about the structure of your essay – and to let the reader know that structure. Clear, strong, structure is important in two respects. First, it helps you, the writer. In the last section I wrote about the importance of having something to say, something interesting. That can be a challenge; it's not easy to find something interesting in every topic on the law course. One way you can help yourself find interest in the material is through clear presentation of your, and other people's, arguments. Forcing yourself to set things out in a clear, sensible order will help you spot problems. If you find your language is becoming vague or evasive, this may be because there is a problem in that area of law, a difficulty that you can help solve. Ask yourself why you are struggling to explain it; is it just a matter of needing to re-read the set texts, or is your difficulty a symptom of something more interesting? If so, explaining and resolving the difficulty may, in itself, provide the core of your essay. Second, a clear structure helps your reader. All essays should have a strong introduction that explains the question they are addressing and which sets out a plan for its resolution, a middle which is divided into a series of sensibly ordered paragraphs, each making a defined point, and a conclusion that draws it all together. It should be easy to read, and the reader should know from the outset what you are arguing and where you are heading. A well-structured exam essay is likely to lead to a happy and grateful examiner.

The Rule of Three

There are lots of good ways of structuring an essay, or arguments within an essay, but, if you are in doubt, three-stage arguments are often helpful. Here are a couple of examples. Some law essays work well as: (1) problem; (2) flawed proposed solutions; (3) my solution. The author sets up a legal difficulty, discusses how others have sought to resolve the problem, but have failed, and concludes by providing a solution that builds on the successes and failures of the second stage. Or how about: (1) the present state of the law with its problems; (2) the causes of these problems; (3) the remedying of these problems, drawing on the causal analysis made in the second stage. This also works for more abstract essays: (1) argument; (2) counter-argument; (3) synthesis. The author sets out an argument, presents the critiques of that argument, and then concludes by defending, or (better still) modifying the initial argument in the face of those critiques. The three-stage model is not the only way to structure things, and might not always be appropriate, but it is a handy tool to have when you are writing an essay and groping for a structure. I suppose it is satisfying because there is: (1) the setting up of the problem; (2) engagement with the problem that fails to bring closure; (3) closure.

Be Nice to Your Villains

Often, perhaps always, you will want to refer to the work of some scholars or judges with whom you disagree. This is part of giving your essay a critical edge. It can be tempting to go in hard, to expose your villains for the fools and rogues that they undoubtedly are, but this is almost always a mistake. Partly, of course, this is just a matter of civility: we shouldn't be rude or mean to people, even if they are academics. But this is also a matter of tactics. If you introduce someone's work in your essay you need to convince the audience that there is a point to the inclusion. If you make your interlocutors sound like idiots, your audience will wonder why you are requiring them to consider their work. Worse, your audience might suspect that you are misrepresenting the interlocutors' work to make it sound silly, or even, worse still, might start to sympathise with the subject of your critique. A far better way to deal with villains is to make their arguments sound as persuasive as possible. Then, when you show the flaws in their reasoning, your audience stays on your side: after all, as you've done the best that can be done to make the reasoning attractive, your subsequent critique of that reasoning appears both fair and decisive.

There you have it. One secret and three tips to help you make use of the secret. Now you need to start writing, and the more you write, the easier it will become. But please, please, once you have become an eminent professor, a senior judge, or the head of the law firm, never forget that poor audience, patiently listening to you.

CHAPTER 16

Guest contribution by Professor Mark Elliott

It is an honour for me to include a contribution by Professor Mark Elliott, Chair of the Faculty of Law at the University of Cambridge, in this book.

Professor Elliott is Professor of Public Law and Chair of the Faculty of Law at the University of Cambridge, and a Fellow of St Catharine's College, Cambridge. From 2015 to 2019, he served as Legal Adviser to the House of Lords Select Committee on the Constitution, providing advice to the Committee on a range of legislative and other matters. He co-founded the international biennial Public Law Conference series and co-convened the first two conferences. He is the recipient of a University of Cambridge Pilkington Prize for excellence in teaching and is the author of a widely read blog, Public Law for Everyone, that is aimed at public law scholars, current and prospective law students, policy-makers, and others who are interested in the subject. I have personally found his blog to be highly instructive and would urge all those interested in public law to read it.

Professor Elliott's contribution below is full of invaluable insights on legal essay writing, and especially for the need to be argumentative. I hope you enjoy reading it.

Writing a Law essay? Remember to argue!

Providing advice in the abstract about how to write Law essays is difficult because so much depends on the nature of the question you are answering. It's also important to take into account whatever are the expectations for your particular course, degree programme or university. Nevertheless, a useful rule of thumb, I think, is that a good Law essay will normally set out and advance a clear thesis or argument. (Note that I'm referring here to essays as distinct from problem questions: the latter call for a different approach.)

The need for an argument

Some answers explicitly call for this. Take, for example, the following essay title:

> 'Do you agree that parliamentary sovereignty is the most important principle in the UK constitution?'

Here, the question itself in effect advances an argument — that parliamentary sovereignty is the most important principle in the constitution — and invites you to say whether you agree with it or not. And in saying whether you agree, you need to advance your own argument: 'I agree with this because…'. Or: 'I disagree because…'. Or even (because if the question advances a position that you think implies a misconception, oversimplification or false premise, you can say so): 'I will argue that the question oversimplifies matters by assuming that a particular constitutional principle can be singled out as uniquely important…'

Other questions may indicate in a less direct way the need for you to put forward your own argument. For example:

> '"Parliamentary sovereignty is the most important principle in the UK constitution." Discuss.'

Here, we don't have a 'do you agree?' prompt; instead, we have the apparently less directive 'discuss' prompt. If we read the question literally, it may seem that there is no need for you to put forward your own argument here. After all, it's possible to 'discuss' something without advancing your own argument about it: you could make various points, explain various matters, and leave the reader to make up their own mind. But while this may be formally true, it's unwise to read the question in this way, because it creates the risk that you will end up writing something very general and descriptive on the topic without going any further.

To summarise, then, there are at least three reasons for making an argument part of your essay. First, the question will often call for this, whether explicitly or implicitly, such that you wouldn't be answering the question if you didn't set out and develop an argument. Second, if you don't impose on yourself the discipline of articulating and defending an argument, you risk underselling yourself by writing something that is descriptive and meandering rather than purposefully constructed. Third, setting out and developing an argument involves taking ownership of the material. By that, I mean using the material in way that serves the purposes of your argument, showing that you are in command of it and that it is not in command of you. This, in turn, provides an opportunity to demonstrate a level of understanding that it would be hard to show in a descriptive essay that simply wandered from point to point.

Setting out your thesis

If putting forward an argument is (often) important or necessary, how should it be done? There are no great secrets here: the formula is straightforward. You should begin your essay by stating your thesis — that is, by setting out what it is that you are going to argue. This should be done in your introductory paragraph — by the time the reader reaches the end of that paragraph, they should be in no doubt about what you are going to argue. Imagine, for instance, that you are presented with the following essay title:

"'The courts have expanded their powers of judicial review beyond all acceptable constitutional limits in recent decades;

it is time to clip the judges' wings." Discuss.'

In response to such a question, it might be tempting to say in your introduction that (for example) you are going to 'show' how the courts' powers of judicial review have grown, 'consider' why this has happened and 'examine' the criticisms of judicial over-reach that have resulted. These are all perfectly sensible things to do when writing an essay on this topic, but if that all you say in your introduction, you will leave the reader wondering what you think — and what you are going to argue. In contrast, an introductory paragraph that lays the foundation for essay that properly advances a thesis will set out what that thesis is. You might, for instance, take each of the propositions set out in the question and stake out your position:

'In this essay, I will argue that (a) while the courts' powers of judicial review have grown in recent decades, (b) it is misguided to suggest that this has breached "all acceptable constitutional limits" and (c) that those who now advocate "clip[ping] the judges' wings" misunderstand the role of the judiciary is a rule of law-based constitution. In other words, the courts' judicial review powers are entirely appropriate and those who seek to limit them risk undermining the rule of law.'

An introduction of this nature would achieve two things. First, it would make clear to the reader the position you proposed to take. Second, it would immediately lend the essay a structure.

Developing your thesis

Once you have set out your thesis in the introduction, you need to develop or defend it. This will involve making a series of connected points in successive paragraphs, each of which relates to your overarching thesis. One way of thinking about this is that the individual points you make in the main body of the essay should all relate or point back in some way — and in a clear way — to the position that you staked out in the introduction.

In the example introduction above, the overarching thesis is set out in the second sentence; the individual and connecting parts of the argument are set out in propositions (a), (b) and (c) in the first sentence. One approach, therefore, would be to divide the answer, once the introduction has been written, into three parts, dealing in turn with points (a), (b) and (c). Naturally, as you work through the various parts of your argument, you will need to cite relevant evidence (cases, legislation, literature and so on) in support of your argument. You will also need to deal with matters that appear, at least at first glance, to sit in opposition to your argument (on which see further below) or which, once properly considered, require your argument to be refined.

A key point, however you proceed, is that the reader should also be clear about how each successive point relates not only to the previous point but also to the overarching argument. The reader should never be left wondering 'Where does this fit in?' or 'Why am I being told this?' A simple way of avoiding these problems is to signpost, by saying at the beginning of each section how it relates to the overall argument. The flipside of this coin is that you should avoid saying things like 'Another point is that…' since this gives the impression, rightly or wrongly, that the various points in your essay have been thrown together in a random order, with little thought as to how they fit together or relate to your overall argument. Even if that's not the case, you don't want to risk giving the reader that impression.

A one-sided approach?

The advice set about above might seem to imply that I'm suggesting you write one-sided essays — in which you set out points that support your argument while ignoring those that don't. However, that's not at all what I'm suggesting. In order to set out your argument in a persuasive manner, you need to deal both with relevant points that support your argument and with relevant points that appear to challenge your argument — and, in dealing with the latter points, you need to show why they do not in fact fatally undermine your argument. In other words, the approach I'm suggesting here doesn't mean that you should adopt a blinkered approach, paying no attention to counterarguments: rather, you need to deal with them in a way that shows that, having thought about and weighed them in the balance, you are in a position to show why your argument stands in spite of them (or why your argument can be adapted in a way that accommodates such points).

All of this points towards a further matter: namely, that advancing an argument in your essay does not mean that you need to (or should) be argumentative in the sense of adopting a strident tone that brooks no debate or compromise. Rather, advancing an argument in the way I've suggested here means being thoughtful and persuasive: taking the reader with you on a journey that demonstrates that you have looked at the relevant material, carefully thought through the issues raised by the question, and arrived at a view that you are able to justify and defend through well-reasoned and suitably evidenced argument.

So what about your conclusion? If you've followed my advice above, it should more or less write itself. People often agonise over conclusions, perhaps thinking that there has to be some 'big reveal' at the end of their essay. But there doesn't need to be and indeed there shouldn't be — any big reveal. There should be no surprises at the end precisely because you've set out your argument at the beginning and spent the rest of the essay carefully constructing the different strands of your argument. The conclusion is an opportunity to draw those stands together, but no-one should have to wait with baited breath for the conclusion before finally realising: 'Ah, so that's what they think!' If that's the effect of your conclusion, it means there's something wrong with the introduction!

CHAPTER 17

Guest contribution by Professor Alison Young

It is an honour for me to include a contribution by Professor Alison Young, the Sir David Williams Professor of Public Law at the University of Cambridge, in this book.

Professor Young is a Fellow of Robinson College, Cambridge and an Emeritus Fellow of Hertford College, Oxford. She currently co-edits the UKCLA blog on constitutional law, and is a member of the Editorial Board of European Public Law, and of Public Law. She is also a Fellow of the Higher Education Academy and a trustee of The Constitution Society. She is affiliated with the Oxford Human Rights Hub and with the Programme for the Foundations of Law and Constitutional Government, both at the University of Oxford.

She conducts research in all aspects of public law, both of the UK and the EU. Her main interest is in constitutional theory, particularly dialogue theory, where she draws comparisons between different means of protecting human rights. She is also interested in comparative public law, specifically drawing comparisons between UK law, EU law, the law in other commonwealth countries and France.

Professor Young's contribution below draws an original (and humorous!) analogy between essay writing and...choosing a film!

I am sure you will enjoy reading it.

Why writing an essay is like choosing a film

We often receive the same advice about how to write a law essay. Any legal essay is an argument. The argument must answer the question you have been given – not one that you would prefer to have been asked. And the question is never; 'please tell me what you have read'; or, more worryingly, 'please write a précis of your textbook and lectures as quickly as possible by the deadline'.

It's also important that the reader can follow your argument. Structure is crucially important. As is signposting, indicating to your reader why you are referring to a case, or an article, or a blog post, to help make your argument. Your introduction sets out the argument you are going to make. Each paragraph develops that argument. Your conclusion relates your argument to the wider context. What does your argument tell us about this area of the law more generally, or about the relationship between law and morality, or between law and politics? The more you write, the more you begin to develop your own style, often from reading articles that do — or do not — provide good examples of how to make an argument and using them to help you structure your own arguments and find your own voice.

The reason you keep reading this advice is because it is true. But how do we actually write an argument? How do we know what side to choose when making an argument? How can we signpost an argument to the reader if we are unsure of the argument we want to make?

How do I make an argument?

A lot of this is a process of learning to be critical and to reflect on your reading. Again, easy to say – but not always easy to do. Each of us uses a different process and sometimes we can use a different process for different essays. My students are probably all too familiar with the whiteboard in my college office. I like to use a brainstorming process. I think of relevant facts, or arguments I've read. When I see them collated on a whiteboard it can be easier to find what I want to say. I start to see themes, begin to reflect on connections between cases and arguments. I will spot common assumptions that I don't agree with or reflect on the consequences of different arguments. I also use mind-mapping software if I'm not near my whiteboard. When I use a similar process with my students, they realise that we can make a range of different good arguments in response to the same question – another valuable lesson to learn when it comes to writing a legal essay.

But this process can still feel a little alien and confusing, especially when you are new to studying law, or new to studying a particular area of law. I want you to take a step back and think about it in a different way. Sometimes that can help us reflect on our own writing, particularly when we are new to studying law.

Should I watch this film?

I want you to imagine a conversation between friends. They're trying to decide which movie to watch as a reward for finally writing that law essay a day before the deadline. They've stumbled across the 2020 adaptation of Emma. One friend has seen the film before but does not mind watching it again. The others want to know whether they should watch the film.

The conversation goes something like this – with editorial asides in square brackets.

> Friend 1: Charlie, you've seen Emma, should we watch it?

> Charlie: Well, it was released in 2020, so it's quite a recent film. It stars Anna Taylor-Joy and Johnny Flynn as Emma and Mr Knightley and there are good performances from Bill Nighy and Miranda Hart…

> Friend 2 (a little angrily): Stop. Boring. That's not helping. You're just telling me facts about the film. But you're not telling me why we should watch the film!

[Please answer the question!]

Charlie: Well…(accessing the internet)…Rotten Tomatoes gave it 86%. Metacritic gave it 71%. One critic even says that 'it's a wondrous retelling of a timeless literary masterpiece'. That's got to be good, right?

Friend 3 (sighs audibly): OK. So they think it's a decent film. But you've seen the film. What did you think?

[Make an argument!]

Charlie (thinks for a while): There are pros and cons. On the plus side, it's a light-hearted and funny film. The staging is really good and it sets the scene well. There are some nice songs running through it. Did I mention those great cameos from Bill Nighy and Miranda Hart? And, in the end, the nice bloke gets the girl, who becomes a better person. On the downside, the film does not strictly stick to the plot of the book. Not all of the events happen in the same order as the book. There are things in the film that do not happen in the book, and there is too much emphasis perhaps on the 'sugary' side of the story.

Friend 1 (looking a bit frustrated): I guess that helps a bit more. But it was a bit 'clinical'.

Friend 2 (angrily): I still think you're telling me facts – only this time it's 'facts about the pros and cons'. I don't know whether I'm supposed to watch the film.

Friend 3 (sighs more loudly): I still don't know what you really think.

Friend 1 (looking even more frustrated): I'm still confused. I've no idea whether I should watch the film or not. You've not really guided me at all!

[Structure, structure, structure! And don't forget to evaluate arguments, don't just set them out!]

Charlie (by this stage a little nervous, and not just about the answer to this question but also about the recently-finished law essay. Sighs deeply and remembers the tutor's comments on an earlier essay): Here goes. I think you would enjoy the film, because you want to watch the film to have an enjoyable evening and not watch it as literary critics or as Austen-purists. I accept that the film does not strictly follow the plot of the book and that some events happen out of order, and that things are added in that were not in the book at all. However, I would argue that these do not detract from the enjoyment of the film. In fact, I would argue that they even enhance it. They help to portray on film the deeper societal critiques you find in the book. They also help you empathise a little more with Emma's character, drawing home the pettiness of her environment and the challenges of living with and caring for some of the characters in the book. I accept that Emma is, perhaps, portrayed a little more sympathetically than in the book, but the film still shows her flaws and does not hold back on the criticism of her follies. It is true that the boy does get the girl in the end. However, the witty dialogue means this is no run-of-the-mill romantic comedy. Moreover, both learn from each other about the meaning of real love and friendship and its value over and above the expectations of society. So, all in all, there's something there for both the casual viewer and the Austen-purist, as the film gently encourages us to reflect on whether views of class, the role of women in society, and our ideals of romantic as opposed to realistic love and friendship really have changed over time.

[There you go – you've structured this as an argument, sign-posting each stage of your argument, used facts to back up your argument and even pointed out a potential larger implication of your argument].

Friend 2 (stroppily): Fine – I didn't want an essay!

Friend 1: I'll get some popcorn and put on the film.

Charlie: I've seen the film. I'm sure you will enjoy it. But I'm off to rewrite the law essay – I'm not sure I gave an argument in response to that question after all…

This may sound a little odd. But sometimes odd examples can help us to think more critically about how we approach things. If this also sounds familiar, it is because this learning process is one that we all go through. So much so that educational theorists have a name for it: the SOLO taxonomy.

I'm off to watch Emma – or maybe rewrite that tricky law article that is sitting on my laptop.

CHAPTER 18

Guest contribution by Professor David Kershaw

It is an honour for me to include a contribution by Professor David Kershaw, Dean of the Law School of the London School of Economics, in this book.

Professor Kershaw is one of the most highly regarded law professors in the field of UK and US corporate law. He is also the General Editor of the Modern Law Review and an Associate Tenant at Cornerstone Barristers. He is admitted to the New York Bar and is a qualified UK solicitor. He holds a LLM and SJD from Harvard Law School and a LLB from the University of Warwick.

His contribution below is full of invaluable insights on legal essay writing.

LEGAL ESSAY WRITING

Legal essays, particularly in examinations, often ask you to discuss or evaluate a statement or claim by another person or your professor. In these types of essay, I find it helps to think about the answer as a structured, evidence-based conversation or debate with the statement. The statement or claim will have several component parts, each one of them needs to be evaluated. Commonly, the different components of the statement provide a ready-made structure for your answer. Let the question lead you to this structure; use it to identify the different sections and headings of your answer. Law is a structured discipline; the question is structured, make sure you use that structure.

In this type of question, it is not uncommon for students to treat the statement simply as an invitation to discuss a particular area of the law, and to show-case their knowledge, without close regard to the claims the statement makes. Such an approach is a mistake. The knowledge and understanding you have must be deployed to interrogate the veracity of each component part of the statement. What arguments and evidence can be marshalled to support the claim? What arguments and evidence are available to problematise the claim that is being made? Bring them both to bear, in an ordered and structured way, in order to reach a conclusion on the claim(s) being made.

What is particular difficult in this process is finding the right relationship between the evidence from legal sources and arguments made by commentators, on the one hand, and your own voice on the other. Too much voice and opinion and it can feel like the evidence is being moulded and even distorted by opinion and political preference. And yet, your voice is essential to a good essay. We want to hear why you think the statement, or a part thereof, is right or wrong or a mixture of the two. Just make sure that your strong voice is built on the arguments and evidence that you deploy.

Finally, a note about introductions. A good essay, we have long been told, has an introduction and a conclusion. But a word of caution on them. It's not always the case with an "evaluate" question that you need much of introduction at all. And when one is useful, students often spend far too long on them. Legal essays will involve word limits or time constraints and there is often a lot to say. Sometimes you need to "cut quickly to the chase" of the detailed argument / "the conversation with the statement". Don't dwell too long on the introduction leaving insufficient space or time for the argument.

CHAPTER **19**

Guest contribution by Professor Joanne van der Leun

It is an honour for me to include a contribution by Professor Joanne van der Leun in this book.
Professor Van der Leun joined Leiden University in 2001 and was one of the pioneering staff members of the Criminology BA and MA program at Leiden Law School and has held various managerial positions.

She was previously affiliated with Utrecht University (where she also received her MSc.) and Erasmus University (where she also received her PhD). She is active in the Dutch Social Science Humanities council. Her research focuses on Crime and Migration including Human Trafficking and Crime policies. She supervises eight PhD students in these areas and loves to write.

Her contribution below is full of invaluable insights on legal essay writing, how to get inspired and how to avoid plagiarism. I am sure you will enjoy reading it!

Get Inspired

Inspiration is everywhere. This holds true for photography, music and also for academic writing. "Get inspired by what others do or have done" is one of the best pieces of advice I received during my own academic career.

There are many styles of academic writing. Developing your own style in writing legal (or criminological or any other) essays can be difficult. Yet, you don't always have to find your own path by digging into your own soul or by patiently waiting till you suddenly invent the wheel. Regularly spending time in the library and online to be inspired by examples you like has proven to be very helpful. When I started to write in English (whereas Dutch is my first language) I kept a little journal in which I noted sentences I liked and thought I could use later on. Not to copy them, but to make them my own and to expand my vocabulary. When I wrote my PhD dissertation, I consciously studied the structure of dozens of other theses, in order to find out what I liked and what did not appeal to me.

Whenever I share this advice with students I immediately notice some nervousness. Students tend to be nervous about potential plagiarism. At first this surprised me. Most educational institutions nowadays explain to their students what plagiarism is and how to prevent it. There are codes of conduct, software is widely used to prevent and spot plagiarism. All institutions have sanctions in place which are applied more strictly than years ago. Every student knows this. So why this uneasiness?

It may be the case that you start copy-and-pasting because you are under pressure as a result of bad planning (this is what many professors think). But I think if you are afraid of plagiarizing unintendedly something else is going on. It seems more likely that you believe you have to reproduce the knowledge of others, the so-called experts, when writing essays. They seem to know everything and you just seem to be struggling, even when you know the citation rules.

What is plagiarism? Most people agree that plagiarism is a form of theft that has to do with not paying enough respect to the work of others. Still, there is a lack of a universally accepted definition and concrete cases can be difficult to judge. Ellis et al. (2018:1) define plagiarism as the practice of "presenting someone else's words and/or ideas as your own without appropriate attribution." Maybe some students, especially when they start writing essays, do not thoroughly understand why it is fine to be inspired by the structure of sentences and even whole manuscripts whereas you run into trouble if you copy & paste ideas of others without the right citations. And maybe professors think too quickly that students know the rules and therefore are able to obey them.

Over the years, I have come to think that the real issue is often a lack of insight into how to write without relying too much on the experts. Once you are confident enough about your own writing, and when you realize that your own reasoning is what matters to your essay, your worries about plagiarism will probably fade.

How to get there? The best way to become more confident is to be aware of the culture and craft of academic (legal) writing. You can develop this by reading in a very different way. If you are now primarily looking for the knowledge that others present in books, articles and case law, I would invite you to (also) look at the literature and secondary sources as a tool to improve your own writing skills. Consciously try to understand what the authors have done in terms of writing and rhetoric, what you like about it and not. Improve your skills by rewriting – in your own style – what you have learned and how your thoughts develop.

The cliché is true: writing is like a muscle. You have to exercise this muscle regularly to develop it and keep it in shape. But you also have to understand and feel which muscle you are training. As long as you truly remember you are exercising this muscle in order to express your own ideas, observations and conclusions, you will start to rely more on your own skills and realize you are not writing to reproduce what others say. Be confident enough to get inspired.

CHAPTER 20

Guest contribution by Professor Catherine Barnard

It is an honour for me to include a contribution by Professor Catherine Barnard in this book, who is a Professor of European & Employment Law at the University of Cambridge and British Academy Fellow.

Professor Barnard is widely regarded as one of the most prominent EU law scholars. Her definitive work includes "The Substantive Law of the EU: The Four Freedoms (OUP, 2019)" and (with Prof. Peers) "European Union Law (ed) (OUP, 2020)".

She has appeared extensively on the main media channels – BBC, ITV and Sky – as well as some of the more specialist programmes such as Law in Action, Woman's Hour and the Briefing Room. She has also written for the Guardian and the Telegraph. She has given evidence to numerous select committees on the legal issues connected with Brexit, immigration and the European Union (Withdrawal) Act.

Her contribution contains lots of invaluable insights, and it provides students with the perspective of both the examiner and the examinee. Enjoy!

Practical Exam Advice

Being examiner on a university exam paper is stressful. Not as stressful as for those sitting them, granted, but stressful none the less. Is the paper fair? Do the problem questions work? Do the questions reflect the syllabus? Are the questions challenging enough to distinguish the best students? Is the language clear? Is there sufficient diversity in the question?

Huge amounts of time and resource are devoted to setting exam papers. Depending on the faculty, one person might hold the pen or a team of people may contribute. There's usually a meeting to discuss the paper with subject specialists and a further meeting of challenge by non-specialists. The polishing continues.

And then there is the small matter of marking the papers and ranking the students.

Generally, law exams contain two types of questions: problem style and essay style.

Problem-style questions

Problem-style questions come with their own built-in structure, especially the ones which are subdivided into parts (a), (b), (c) etc. For the ones that are not, the best advice is to begin by identifying the potential claimants and the defendants and their various claims and defences. Use some subheadings to show that you have identified the major issues and to establish a structure for your response which it will be easy for the examiner to follow.

And then there is the questions of remedies. I always suggest that students put themselves in the shoes of the claimant. What does the Claimant want out of the claim? Declaration? Damages? Injunction? In EU law exams it is always helpful to think too about the routes to get there. Is it cheaper and better to complain to the Commission to see if it can intervene (restrictive national law may get repealed but no damages) or is it better to go to the national court and rely on the directly effective right (no longer possible in the UK but still possible in certain limited circumstances in Northern Ireland) and possibly get damages? By thinking around these questions, the student shows that they can use their legal reasoning to understand not only the theory but also the practical implications of the law.

Essay questions

Essay questions are generally more challenging. First, you need to have something to say about the topic other than the most obvious. Have you read some academic literature on the subject which you can make effective use of? Second, which follows from the first, do you have a 'thesis' or argument. This is a major departure from a school essay. This thesis allows you to express something of your own views, to have an opinion about the law and to say something interesting; examiners like this.

So, take a general essay title e.g. 'The Charter of Fundamental Rights has failed to deliver on its promise of individual rights protection. Discuss'. What do you think? What's your argument? Avoid 'on the one hand…on the other'; don't be ambivalent, take a stance. For instance, your argument might be that you disagree, that the Court (ECJ) has striven to protect individual rights and has done so successfully, but that in so doing has stretched the boundaries of the competence of EU law and brought into question its own legitimacy. This thesis then shapes the essay that follows: e.g. para 1 sets out your argument and how you are going to make that argument. Paras 2 – 6 consider what the Charter says about individual rights, and how the Court has developed the protection of these rights. Use carefully selected examples (e.g. cases like Portuguese judges, WABE, Bauer as compared to Alemo Herron; you don't need to be comprehensive). Paras 7-9 discuss concerns about 'competence creep' and criticism of the Court (perhaps citing the concerns of the Polish and German Constitutional courts); para 10 concludes by summarising what you have done.

Finally, some general points:

1. ABQ (answer the bloody question)

2. Write simple, clear English (if you don't think you write well, read The Economist for a while)
3. Use sub-headings
4. Underline case names
5. Have evidence/source/citation for each point made
6. Cite academic literature where appropriate

And remember that examiners are human beings – probably tired ones – so if the exam answer is done by hand, try to make it as legible as you possibly can.

Good luck.

CHAPTER **21**

Guest contribution by Professor Stephen Weatherill

It is an honour for me to include a contribution by Professor Stephen Weatherill in this book.

Professor Weatherill was the Jacques Delors Professor of European Law from January 1998 until September 2021, since when he holds that title Emeritus. He also served as Deputy Director for European Law in the Institute of European and Comparative Law, and was a Fellow of Somerville College.

Professor Weatherill, or Steve as he insisted I call him, was my doctoral supervisor in Oxford. He is an inspiration to me and to all of his students. His apparent omniscience on all matters EU law, coupled with his incredible modesty, made my doctoral journey more enjoyable than I could have reasonably hoped for.

Below you will find his essay-writing advice to law students. Do pay attention! His experience and insights are invaluable. Here we go…

Answer the question!

How trivial that sounds. Of course you are expected to answer the question. Who wouldn't understand that?

You'd be surprised.

Guest contribution by Professor Stephen Weatherill

In thirty-five years of marking tutorial essays and examination scripts I suspect I've seen it all. Errors, misunderstandings, illogicality, misrepresentations ... and, let me be quick to add, plenty of soaring brilliance, deep engagement, perceptive analysis and agile analogies too. But what's the one instruction that drives me to distraction when it's neglected?

Answer the question!

Everyone gets things wrong. Maybe because you don't fully understand it, maybe because you could have spent a bit longer in the library and a bit less time watching the football, maybe because it's a really tough issue. Fine. You'll get some bits wrong, you'll get some – most, we hope – things right, and you'll get more-or-less the grade that your level of knowledge reflects.

But that's not true of the student who doesn't answer the question. If you don't answer the question you are immediately stopping yourself achieving your potential.

Look, I know it's tempting. You've worked hard on studying the matter of how far the

Charter of Fundamental Rights is treated as capable of application to private parties. You've read the case law, you've read the academic analysis. More than that, you're bursting with normative enthusiasm, you have shaped your own pet theory of where and when horizontal application should be embraced, and your seminar leader has praised you for your insight and ambition. So you eagerly turn over your examination paper and you spot the question about the Charter, and you start writing with feverish glee. It's a question about the extent to which measures taken at Member State level are subject to review in the light of the standards mandated by the EU's Charter, but never mind, you know what you want to write about and it's not that, and so you reel off your elegant essay on horizontal application.

Don't do it.

Answer the question!

A wonderful answer to a question that has not been asked scores a lower mark than a competent answer to a question that has been asked.

And you won't get extra marks for artistic impression. It's a Law examination not a figure skating competition.

Answer the question!

Think about it from the perspective of the person(s) who set the examination paper. We don't knock these out in ten minutes just before the Champions League anthem booms forth while waiting for the pizza to come bubbling out of the oven. Setting an exam paper is not exactly a source of joy but it is a matter of professional pride, and hours are invested by a team of people to ensure the paper is fair, balanced, accurate and appropriately challenging. Each question is crafted like Meissen porcelain. And if we have – after careful reflection and judicious choice – directed you to discuss a quote criticising the Court's unwillingness to entertain preliminary references submitted by arbitral tribunals we really do not want to read your thoughts on the modern status of the CILFIT guidelines. No matter how brilliant your insights on that issue might be.

So ... answer the question.

CHAPTER 22

Conclusion: It's not all about the marks

I know why you have read this book: you want to improve your marks! It's only natural. I wanted to get the best marks too, to graduate top of my class too. I succeeded, but only after I succeeded did I realise that it's not all about the marks…

Think of it this way. Why do you actually want to get good marks? Is it because you have been conditioned to pursue good marks from the day you were born as a metric of self-worth? That's probably it, is it not?

That's fine. That's, to an extent, normal. In any case, how you were raised and what the educational system instilled in you is not your fault.

However, I am sure that, growing up, you realised that more things matter in life than the mark you got at Uni. You see people that did not do well in school excel in all walks of life and in every single respect. They are wealthy, healthy, have great families etc. Thus, it becomes clear that marks are not the single best determinator of your future success and happiness. Take it easy. Don't burn out chasing that extra 1%. It is important, but not as much as you think.

You might ask: why are you, the author of this book which shows students how to achieve better marks, so cool about marks?

It is easy for you to say: you actually did get good marks!

Well, it is exactly because I am saying it that you should value it. If someone who is not wealthy tells you that wealth is not that crucial, you would be right to object: how would you know? However, if a wealthy individual discredits wealth, you are more likely to take them seriously. They are not incentivized to denigrate, for no good reason, what they spent many years pursuing. They might have something important to say; listen to them.

I would, thus, like to conclude by asking you to be patient and not obsess over marks. Do what you can to improve them, but no more. Don't ruin your health or you relationships over marks.

Please keep the following in mind:

- Doing badly in an exam is not the end of the world. Exams do not and will not define your future success in life or (more importantly) your happiness.

- Be kind to yourself. You can always (in theory) study more, revise more efficiently, read more cases. However, in truth, there is both a physical and a psychological limit and your body/mind will start complaining when you cross it. Listen to its voice.

- Try to enjoy this period of time and the exam process, if at all possible. View exams as your opportunity to showcase your hard work, not as a make-or-break moment.

- Keep calm and carry on. This too shall pass and you will only emerge stronger and more experienced.

Do your best, but no more than that.
Best of luck with your essays!

CHAPTER 23

About the Author

My name is Dimitrios Kyriazis. I am an Assistant Professor of EU Law at the Law School of the Aristotle University of Thessaloniki and a Member of the Associated Researchers Group of the European Banking Institute. I am also a Research Fellow in Law at Northeastern University London (formerly New College of the Humanities – NCH), where I previously served as Head of the Law Faculty and Senior Lecturer in Law (2017-2020). I joined NCH in 2017, having taught for several years at Oxford University on the undergraduate and postgraduate degrees, first as a tutor and then as a Lecturer in Law. I served as Teaching Fellow in Law at UCL and I have delivered guest lectures at Leiden University, Queen Mary University of London, Lund University and IE Law School. I continue to deliver guest lectures on Oxford's postgraduate programmes.

I am the Founding Partner of Kyriazis Law Offices in Athens and I have previously practiced law in Brussels (Freshfields Bruckhaus Deringer LLP) and Athens (Bernitsas Law), primarily working on State Aid, M&A and Competition Law. Since 2020, I have been running "The Law Prof" blog, trying to help students with actionable essay writing advice: https://www.thelawprof.com/.

I obtained my LLB (Distinction) at the University of Athens, graduating top of my class. I also hold an MJur (Distinction) from the University of Oxford, graduating top of my class

(Clifford Chance Prize for the best overall performance in the MJur), with the support of an Onassis Foundation scholarship.

I completed my MPhil in Law (Distinction) as a Light Senior Scholar at St Catherine's College in Oxford. Finally, I completed my DPhil (PhD) at Oxford University, with the support of a Clarendon scholarship, an Onassis scholarship, and a grant from the UK Chartered Institute of Taxation. The Clarendon scholarship is arguably the most competitive scholarship of Oxford University; according to its official description, when 'selecting Clarendon scholars, the University has only one goal in mind: to choose the best students worldwide, as decided by experts in each student's field.'